$\mathcal{U}$NDERSTANDING AND RESEARCHING SCRIPTS

A Practical Guide

UNDERSTANDING AND RESEARCHING SCRIPTS

A Practical Guide

John Hester

THE CROWOOD PRESS

First published in 2006 by
The Crowood Press Ltd
Ramsbury, Marlborough
Wiltshire SN8 2HR

www.crowood.com

British Library Cataloguing-in-Publication Data
A catalogue record for this book is available from the British Library.

ISBN 1 86126 780 0
EAN 978 1 86126 780 1

Photograph previous page: from *Julius Caesar*. Photograph by Robbie Jack.

Typeset by D & N Publishing
Lambourn Woodlands, Hungerford, Berkshire.

Printed and bound in Great Britain by Biddles Ltd, King's Lynn, Norfolk.

Contents

UNDERSTANDING AND RESEARCHING SCRIPTS ENSEMBLE

Brighton Dome Youth Theatre

Shona Bland
Neil Faulkner
Nicole-Faye Head
Amy Holmes
Jamie Langlands
Sarah Musk
Chris Nunn
Offue Okegbe

Saskia Roddick
Charles Shetcliffe
Chris Tibble
Anna Walseth
Bethany Warren
Hattie Windsor
Brendan Wyer
Louie Young

DEDICATION

To Miss King (Alison) – a much valued colleague and friend.

ACKNOWLEDGEMENTS

A special thank you to my father who looked after business while I was writing this book and to Tina Bicât who suggested that I write about drama in the first place. A very special thank you also to Inservice Productions, to my cousin Penny Cobbold (one of their resident professionals) for organizing the photographs and to the director Priyanga Burford for allowing her very talented young actors to be photographed in rehearsal. All those involved with Inservice Productions and Brighton Dome Youth Theatre are shining examples of what can be achieved when committed performers and a play get together.

INTRODUCTION

The aim of this book is to provide a practical guide to approaching a play with a view to its eventual production. As such, although there is much emphasis upon researching a text and analysing its contents, it is not an attempt to facilitate an academic study of drama. While this is a noble pursuit and one that may be interesting to study elsewhere, it is not of immediate concern in these pages. Rather, it is assumed that you are reading this book, not because you wish to achieve a theoretical understanding of a script, but because you are motivated by a desire to find a practical approach to unravelling its complexities in a way that will enable you to bring it to performance in an imaginative and truthful manner.

In the same way that the writer of a play feels excitement and anticipation when preparing to put 'pen to paper', so is it immensely exciting for an actor or director to be faced with the resulting work, charged with the onerous responsibility of nurturing it towards its next stage of existence – that is a living, three-dimensional interpretation of it.

However, theatrical interpretation can become a very haphazard process. In a rush to be interesting, imaginative, innovative, dynamic and exciting it is very easy to lose focus and forget that the text itself should remain the primary resource and arbiter between the performer and playwright.

This book will teach you how to interpret a play methodically and organically, and will encourage performances that grow naturally out of the text and then develop, using your skills of interpretation in harmony with the play and its intentions.

There are, of course, a large number of people usually engaged in any theatrical production, employed in a variety of important roles and functions. This book will focus mainly upon actors and directors, but despite this, it should also prove a useful insight into understanding text for all other members of a production team.

Although an actor's approach to a play is different in many ways from a director's, there are also, of course, many similarities and it is the intention of this book not to be too separatist in its approach to guiding both. The relationship between actor and director should be co-operative and mutually dependant, and it is the philosophy here to encourage this within the process of interpretation. Where it is necessary to differentiate between the techniques employed by actors and directors the book will not hesitate to do so and elucidate both. However, where possible, the two roles will be seen as one in terms of approaching the text and understanding the means of its performance. In this way, the book should not only be of immense use to both but will encourage, from the outset, an emphasis upon the importance of the partnership.

To this end, and to avoid confusion, the term *Theatre Practitioner* will be used throughout all the chapters. Although this clearly refers to all the various members of a production team, it will mainly and in particular refer to actors and directors for the purposes of the book. However, it is hoped that an insight will be provided for all theatrical personnel into the work required to faithfully represent an author's work upon the stage, as well as encouraging a mutual respect amongst everyone involved in the process.

There are many techniques and processes involved in 'understanding text', but most of them fall under two very broad category headings. These are 'research' and 'analysis'. Because of this, these two terms are referred to often and are used as a way of focusing attention upon, not only the differences between the two, but also the similarities. Although they may be arbitrarily separated on many occasions, it should be remembered that they are really very much 'two sides of the same coin' – that is, very basic definitions within a complete whole that is 'interpretation'. Neither are they totally inclusive, as not all of the techniques needed to understand text fall neatly under their categorization. However, they should serve as a way of enabling you to identify clearly the two processes, develop the skills required for them both and then skilfully practise them in an holistic and inclusive fashion.

As you work through the book you will find that particular plays are referred to as both examples and an opportunity to practise what you have learned. Make sure that you become familiar with all of these and use them as an opportunity, not only to put the skills you are learning into practice, but to also increase your knowledge of dramatic literature. Where a playwright is mentioned, read as many of his or her plays as possible, and consider how you would research, analyse and interpret them. The mind of a Theatre Practitioner should be constantly active and the more widely you read the more instinctively you will be able to apply yourself to the interpretational requirements of the various types of drama to be encountered.

You will also find that some particular plays are quoted in the text. Use these as exercises in the way that is detailed for each of them, but remember also to search out and read the plays in full. The more information about drama that you have at your disposal the better will be your ability to make it live upon the stage; this is true both in general and in particular.

This then is an opportunity not only to realize the full potential of the Theatre Practitioner, but also that of the playwright. As will soon become clear, each is uniquely dependent upon the other. It is the responsibility of everyone involved in theatre to do their very best and give of themselves one hundred per cent in their theatrical endeavours. This responsibility, in practice, begins and ends with the written word (the play). However, in between, there is a fascinating and inspirational journey to be taken. This is a journey of understanding, interpretation and realization. The book will teach you to travel in a constructive and productive way and sojourn safely in the exciting and exotic lands of theatre.

1 THE PROCESS OF DRAMA

THE GENIUS OF DRAMA

It is vital from the outset that you understand the essential difference between drama and other art forms, not in terms of the finished product, which is obvious, but in terms of the process. It is the uniqueness of the very structure of dramatic art that lifts it above its peers and establishes it as a living, breathing, fluid and expanding form that can speak with authority to a wide range of human beings about an equally wide range of topics within the human experience.

In order to fully appreciate this difference you must first consider other art forms and how they work. If you were to paint a picture, write a novel or fashion a sculpture you would be instigating a two-way process between you and your audience. You would create the art, hopefully utilizing a great depth of your own personal thoughts and feelings about the subject matter and, more importantly, doing so in your capacity as a totally unique person: all of your knowledge and experience of the essential 'you' becomes available as source material. Another person looking at, reading or 'experiencing' your creation, in whatever way, would engage themselves in the same manner to discover the meaning of your work for them, how they related to it and, most importantly of all, how it changed their perception and understanding of the subject.

It is in this two-way, but multi-layered, transmission of thoughts, feelings and ideas

OPPOSITE: *Actors play a vital role in the 'three-way process'.*

between artist and recipient that art finds its indispensable place in the world. Through this process you are able to speak to your audience with more depth and complexity than mere direct communication of language would allow; you are able to connect to people you do not know and cannot see. This is not just a connection of minds but of hearts and souls as well. It may well be that your art might inspire a reaction that had not consciously occurred to you at all – this is not a defect of art but its genius. As it passes from its creator to its beneficiary it grows, changes, adapts and somehow develops a life of its own, while still remaining essentially the artist's personal creation.

In light of this, it is not difficult to see how much more the artistic process can flourish in terms of this almost lifelike development and mature if instead of a two-way process between humans it becomes a three-way one. This is drama. There is a creator of the art as before (the playwright) and there are recipients (the audience), but there is also a third party – the facilitators of the work, the people who take the words from the page where the playwright has left them and breathe life and passion into them upon the stage. There is an additional link in the chain of conscious and subconscious communication that liberates and empowers drama beyond the norm of all other art. In other words, between the artist and his or her public there comes the additional mechanism of interpretation and it is the practice of this interpretation that lifts drama to its lofty place of importance within society.

It is to this vocation of interpretation that you, as a theatre practitioner, are called; it is here that you find your place in the scheme of things. You are part of a worldwide community dedicated to employing your talents and skills in order to ensure that this three-way artistic process fulfils its great potential as a priceless form of poetic communication, with its very exciting and stimulating ability to entertain.

THE RESPONSIBILITY OF DRAMA

Within the collaboration between author and practitioner in presenting a finished play to an audience there comes a responsibility on both sides – each to the other. This is quite apart from the obvious duty to produce the best possible work each side is capable of. You will need an understanding of these responsibilities, both yours and the playwright's, before you can successfully begin your job of interpretation.

The author has a responsibility to the practitioner in terms of freely and generously giving up the work for interpretation in the first place. This is an extremely brave and generous requirement, but an essential one nonetheless. A playwright should not try to influence or restrict the practitioner in any way, beyond the structuring of a play as it exists in text form. In a sense this is very much like parenting; the parent gives life to the child, nurtures and develops it, educates and enables it, but then must let it go freely into the world to make its own way and become its own person. Thus must a playwright regard his or her work. The play must be born and raised (honed and tuned), but when it is fully grown it must be allowed to move unhindered into the world of interpretation. As a practitioner you must never forget the sacrifice that an author makes in allowing you to be an equal partner in this artistic enterprise. Neither must they forget that unless the 'gift' is given freely the drama will never fulfil its potential.

Your responsibility stems from that of the author. If this work is to be given freely into your hands, you must reciprocate by remaining faithful to the intentions and priorities of the playwright. This does not mean that you should become their slave or puppet, or that you must not fully and enthusiastically commit all of your artistic 'being' to your interpretation. However, it does mean that you should do so with humility and truth, finding this truth because of the text and not despite it. The better the playwright the easier it will be for you to exercise this responsibility, but you must try to do so to the best of your ability in all circumstances. If you do not, you will not do justice to the work or yourself. Remember that you are a 'steward' of the play not the 'owner' of it. Your stewardship should lead you to bring every bit of your imagination, creativity and ingenuity to the task; it should enable you to enrich, enhance and develop the play unashamedly; but it should not allow you to deface, abuse or disrespect it. Always be truthful to the play, but be brave enough to find this truth in your own honest reading of it.

All of this may be easier said than done, so later you will learn how to faithfully interpret an author's work using your own personality and skill, whilst maintaining integrity and without imposing upon the text.

In the meantime, having established an understanding of these mutual responsibilities, and an appreciation of the unique process of drama, it will now be useful for you to examine each of the three parts of this three-way art form in more detail.

The Play

A play, in itself, is a unique form of fictitious writing. A novel usually contains much descriptive writing, allowing the readers to formulate their own personal reality of the work in their imaginations. A poem does much the same thing but

Performing is a great responsibility.

usually achieves this in a more disparate use of imagery and metaphor that appeals directly to the reader's emotions. However, a play creates a much more definite and, at face value, more communal reality by its use of specific and direct application of words and actions. A play text presents its world in actual terms by providing a blueprint for a performance of something that will be viewed by several or many people at once, as a re-creation of events that are happening 'in the moment' and are accessed by the audience as immediate, tangible and definable representations of reality, within the confines of the subject matter.

It is certainly true that many plays portray an extremely exaggerated, sometimes surreal form of reality, but it is a reality that is designed to be far more defined and embodied when given its easily observed existence upon a stage than a novel or poem may be as it lives alone in the hearts and minds of its readers.

Because a play is written to be performed more than it is to be read, it is, by comparison with other written art forms, less complete and more fractured when viewed upon the page. Here lies the true skill of the playwright. If the play is to be a good one then it must contain just enough information but not too much. If there is not enough substance within the situation and dialogue, not enough information about the characters, not enough action to warrant the type of subject matter, then the theatre practitioners will falter as they struggle to interpret it. However, if it is overwritten, containing too much of its essential ingredients in an over-rich mix then they will become stifled and straitjacketed to the extent of losing their ability to give proper life to the work.

A play text is a fine balancing act and one that must be achieved using mainly dialogue. True, an author may employ copious stage directions if desired but, in a sense, this is irrelevant. If a play is to seem realistic and believable, to give the correct weight to given situations without trivializing them and to achieve an impression of life happening in 'real time', then the amount of dialogue and its consistency must be just right. The best writing is 'economic' in its approach, but it must be economy with substance.

In the same way and for the same reasons, the 'quality' of the dialogue is vitally important. This is partly because the story and situation will stumble in its advance when the dialogue is poor but also, and more importantly, it is extremely hard to identify characters and envisage them as living beings if the lines they are given lack finesse and relevance.

If you admire good playwrights (which, of course, you should), then one of the main areas of your admiration must lie in their ability to create rich and vibrant characters using only the words they speak as building blocks for their construction. A novelist has the luxury of unlimited use of description and narration in order to create and establish a character. However, a dramatist must achieve this using only the words spoken by the character and how they are used. It is true that the job does not need to be as complete as in a novel, for the process of characterization in a play is, of course, shared with the actor playing the part, but this process will only work fully if the writing clearly defines and distinguishes the characteristics required – a very skilful accomplishment using only dialogue.

It must also be remembered that a character in a play must be drawn quickly. Although an audience may expect to learn more about a character as a play progresses, they must also be able to identify them as fully fleshed-out people early on, otherwise they will fail to become engaged with the character's dilemmas within the framework of the play. So much of a playwright's craft centres upon their ability to use dialogue not only to create tension and drama and, perhaps, comedy, but to put down strong and accessible roots of characterization that an actor, with the help of a director, can successfully develop into a fully fledged human being. As a theatre practitioner you will soon learn, if you have not done so already, that the more accomplished a dramatist is in this regard the easier and more fulfilling will become your job.

A good play will also have a strong theme or themes and a clearly defined sense of purpose in the way these are expanded and developed through the course of the action. This central core of the work does not necessarily need to be of a highly artistic or intellectual nature (a play is, after all, primarily designed to entertain and the theme may well revolve strongly around this requirement, as in the case of a thriller or light comedy), but it does need to be designed as a solid and robust framework, around which the play can be built in a full and well-balanced

OPPOSITE: *The importance of the play.*

14

way. Again, it is the quality and execution of these themes that determine the difficulty and enjoyment of the interpretation. A well themed play may prove extremely challenging and rewarding for theatre practitioners, but a poorly themed one can become the opposite.

Interpretation – the Task

As has already been established, it is the interpretation of a play, prior to its reception by an audience, that marks drama out as such a marvellous art form. Thus it becomes obvious that interpretation is of vital importance. Indeed, in terms of any particular performance, interpretation is everything, for a poorly interpreted play will fail at whatever quality level it is written. Actors, directors and their colleagues hold considerable power over the text in their ability to make or break it. The very essence of your job is to summon every ounce of talent and technique you possess in order to make your interpretation as good as it possibly can be.

A badly written play can be salvaged to a certain extent by good interpretation, a mediocre play can be made good, a good play can be made great and a great play can shine brilliantly in all its glory when interpreted in a skilful and imaginative production. On the other hand, if the interpretation is inadequate, a bad play becomes turgid in extremis, a mediocre play seems simply bad and a good play sorely fails to live up to its potential; a great play will always express its greatness in some way, but a bad production will certainly not highlight its attributes.

In fact, a great work of dramatic art requires its interpreters to walk the thinnest of tightropes. Although it provides high-quality source material to fully enable practitioners to excel in their task, it also places much greater responsibility upon the quality of the production as a whole. For instance, Shakespeare's *Macbeth*, when interpreted well, is a play of wondrous breadth and intellectual complexity (despite its refreshingly direct and straightforward plot), but if interpreted badly it can appear farcical and unbalanced; it will still obviously appear to be a great play (Shakespeare has long since passed the stage of having to defend his reputation too vigorously), but the defects of the production will be painfully obvious and, in fact, magnified by the quality of the text. Ironically, it is the greatness of the play that throws most weight of criticism upon the interpretation when the production is poor. There are many top line dramas that can be 'unforgiving' in this way and you should beware of this.

Interpretation – the Process

As your intention in reading this book is to develop your skills in analysing and understanding text, it will be useful at this stage to examine how this will ideally fit into the process of interpretation within a typical rehearsal period for a production. Although this book is not about the rehearsal process as such, but is rather concerned with the study you will undertake within it, it will be helpful in supplying you with a rough model of procedure upon which to base your text work as you start to examine it in greater detail later on. The amount of time available to rehearse a production will vary immensely. Amateur productions may be rehearsed over a period of several months but the cast may only meet once weekly (particularly in the early stages), making the actual hours worked much shorter than one might expect; professional shows can utilize six or seven weeks' full-time, but three or two weeks are much more likely and a one-week rehearsal period is still not uncommon.

Whatever time is at the disposal of you and your colleagues it is vital that you engage in as much preliminary work prior to the commencement of rehearsals as you possibly can. However, remember that, as with so many other things, quality is more important than quantity and it is important that you work in

The importance of the play.

the right way so as to make the very best use of the time you are dedicating to the task.

Although you will hopefully discover your own 'right' way of working effectively upon text and its interpretation as you progress through the chapters of the book, it is worth making one important procedural point at this stage. Do not pre-learn your words before rehearsals start unless it is absolutely necessary, for this can be preparatory work

that is somewhat counterproductive. The reason for this is simple: acting is essentially about finding the thoughts and intentions behind the words and you should therefore learn lines when you are in a position to learn the correct reasons for them being said – learning them 'parrot fashion' can lead to a lifeless interpretation. Of course, if you have only a very short time to rehearse it may be expedient to ignore this rule and make the best of it, but only do so if you have to and, if you are directing, never insist upon actors learning lines before rehearsals start if at all avoidable.

Allied to this is the need for all of your pre-rehearsal study to remain flexible. You should aim to arrive at rehearsals with a good understanding of your character and what the play means to you. However, this knowledge must be seen in terms of being a fluid resource and not as an intractable position of artistic intent. Drama is a communal activity and the whole process of rehearsing should be seen as a journey of discovery that moves towards making final decisions of interpretation at as late a stage as practically possible.

The cast's first meeting is crucial.

The first day of rehearsals should consist of a read-through of the play, an introductory talk by the director, a chance for cast members to see designs of costume, lighting and set, and a discussion of views upon the play at this early stage. All of this preliminary work is vital in establishing the foundations upon which all subsequent endeavours can be built.

The read-through is not particularly important as it gives cast members an opportunity to freely experiment with their thoughts upon the play thus far and get a feeling for what their characters may eventually become. This process has been described as playing a part while 'sitting down' prior to spending the entire rehearsal period learning how to do it

'standing up'. Although the truth of this is dubious, the read-through should certainly be seen as an opportunity to 'throw paint upon a canvas' with the intention of defining and refining 'the brush work' later. If you are directing, reading the whole play through at this stage will pay great dividends and should only be abandoned if you are very dangerously short of time.

From this point onwards, and as the production begins to formulate and take shape, your work upon the text will be divided between the rehearsal sessions and your own personal work at home (or utilizing your time spent travelling on public transport). As you progress, a great deal of your 'homework' will consist of line learning, but remember that the analysis of character and the play must continue throughout the rehearsal and beyond into the performances. You should feel that you never stop learning about the work until the very last performance and, even then, it may well be that you look forward with relish to working on the play again in the future (depending upon its quality, of course).

It must be your responsibility during rehearsals to make sure that you do not get bogged down in the various, more mundane, practicalities that present themselves. Much rehearsal time inevitably becomes taken up with discussions about things such as movement, volume, pace and positioning upon the stage. These are all essential considerations and part of your job, but make sure that you don't neglect the intellectual rigours of interpretation and analysis as you work, and try to compensate for any imbalance of priorities with your personal work and thinking away from the rehearsal room.

Some directors like to 'block' the entire play (determine the basic moves and positions of the characters) first and then move on to the more rigorous task of 'working' through each scene in terms more of understanding and analysis; others determine the blocking more organically as rehearsals progress. Whatever approach is adopted, try not to see blocking purely in practical terms. Your research upon the part and the play will, to an extent, determine the movement employed in the piece and, very often, this can work in reverse, as moving in a certain way, or the physical juxtaposition between characters, can lead to revealing insights of understanding.

One of your most important considerations should be to place all of your own individual work into the context of working with the other members of the company as a team. You cannot allow your interpretation, analysis and research to reach its conclusions unilaterally. Of course this will not apply if your work in this regard is outside of an actual production and your study is directed to a purely academic examination of the text, but when working practically upon a play for performance it is essential to pool your intellectual efforts in order for the production to work as a communal project. If you are directing, your responsibility to foster this approach is obvious, but actors must also be aware that their understanding of character and events must be in tune with the other actors with whom they will be relating so closely and inextricably within the plot of the work.

As the rehearsal period reaches its climax, technical and dress rehearsals will commence. Many actors and directors forget that this is a very important time for the stage managers, designers and technicians as the more practical details of the production are fashioned. Therefore, it is wise for you to have completed the bulk of your work and thinking prior to this stage. If you are reasonably secure in the results of your work upon the text, you are unlikely to be thrown by the rigours and distractions of the sometimes extremely complex technicalities of lights, sound, costumes, scenery and props.

Interpretation – the Relationship between Actor and Director

The relationship between an actor and director is of great importance and, like all worthwhile relationships, must be worked at in order to be totally successful. The interpersonal skills of both are of obvious importance but, in keeping with the preoccupation of this book, you should examine the relationship in terms of the different approach each has with regard to research and analysis. Having established this, it will be easier for you to study the following chapters with a clear understanding of how the various procedures of interpretation may be applied to each of the two roles.

The director needs an overall view of the play in terms of the approach that the production is to take. Before rehearsals even start he or she must have formulated a concept of the work and an angle for executing this in practice. Although this should be an inclusive philosophy it must incorporate a view as to how each of the component parts of the production (especially the characters) will contribute to the framework as a whole. This concept must be strong enough to enable the director to lead the company safely through the rehearsal process, but it must not be inflexible or intractable. A director must enable each actor to play their part effectively within the project as a whole, and an over-rigid attitude to interpretation will stifle this and lead to unproductive instructiveness or even dictatorialness in the communication of ideas.

The directors must also work upon an appreciation of the relevance of each scene to the overall concept. Their work in this regard must be aimed at giving their actors triggers and pointers in finding a productive path through the action and emotional development of the scene. Again, these must all be designed to be implicitly two-way: every observation that a director makes and communicates about the text must be viewed as a

starting point for discussion and further discovery mutually, not as an encumbering edict. However skilful or accurate a director's analysis may be, it will falter and fail in its relevance if it is simply imposed on an equal partner in the process without regard to further opinion and insight.

An actor must work towards a similar all-embracing view of the play, but will also be required to research and analyse their own particular character to a much greater extent. These two factors are not mutually exclusive and, therefore, all the context of an actor's discoveries about the role they are to play must always be set within a concept of the production as a whole. It cannot be stressed enough that this must be seen as a group concept, democratically and co-operatively reached, and all analysis of character and situation must be compatible with that of the other actors and the director.

It is worth noting another major difference between the interpretive approach of an actor and director. A director works towards an understanding and vision of the play that will lead to a group of actors being able to perform it truthfully and effectively. An actor does likewise but from the standpoint of having to bring a character to life personally, utilizing his or her own body, voice and personality in the process. Self-knowledge is paramount here and a good actor will angle his or her work upon the text towards enabling the character to live through their own person rather than despite it. Actors should realize that they must 'find' the part that they are to play in themselves, rather than assuming that they can 'become' another person while maintaining realism. Therefore, their unique, intimate and empathetic understanding of themselves, plus their own invaluable

view of life fashioned from their life experiences, will influence and, indeed, shape their approach to the text and its exploration. This is not to say that an actor should not remain open-minded and objective, but they should also remember to research a script from within themselves as personalities, rather than as an external, academic exercise.

This point emphasizes the importance of the relationship between an actor and a director, and focuses upon the particular responsibility that a director has towards its success. While a director's early research may be happily rooted in personal preference, as rehearsals progress, they should divert much of their efforts to getting to know how their actors think and feel, particularly in relation to the parts they are playing. Their work must start veering towards how an analysis of the text will help and enable particular actors to play particular parts; a director does not have a blank canvas with which to work, but rather particular human beings with specific bodies, voices and souls. While most actors will look to their director to give them a lead in interpretation, they will also expect that the interpretation will be tailored to them and not be a blanket of research that might be applied to any actors or any production.

It is worth a reminder here that most analysis of text, however academically involving it may be, is essentially undertaken for the simple practical purpose of bringing that text to the stage in living glory. An actor will be at 'the sharp end', on stage for each performance long after a director may have gone home or moved on to another project. Nothing focuses a mind more upon the importance of effective research and interpretation than knowing that one must literally 'live' with the results and be judged on them nightly.

The Audience

There is no point in examining the role of an audience in the three-way dramatic process, except in terms of its relevance to you as interpreter. It may be worth remembering from the outset that the audience is the ultimate reason for all of your work upon the text, and their reaction to that work is your every and only motivation. It is not without significance that the part played by the audience is the one factor over which you have no control; ironically though, it is the part for which all of your labours are being expended in your attempt to exert an appreciable influence as you pass the work from the playwright to the audience, laden with honest interpretation.

Undoubtedly, the audience is the 'customer' in this venture. While they have their own particular responsibilities of open-mindedness and fair play, they are not obliged to conform to any rules that you may see as predefined by the quality of the text or your tireless and skilful work upon it. In the same way that a painter cannot demand, or even expect, a particular reaction to a painting, neither must you to an interpretation of a play. There is no right or wrong way for an audience to receive a production, merely 'a way', and you will have been wasting your time if your research on text ignores this fact. An art form remains a fluid, 'living' entity throughout its existence and this includes the time it is received by its recipients and beyond. All of your analysis must be designed to allow you the best possible chance of moving the work productively on to the next stage of the process and, although the audience are very much the junior partners in terms of work input, they must be respected as equal participants if the work is to exist in poetic and artistic terms rather than just simply as a demonstration of craft. This is a professional view of research and analysis in practical terms and it is one that should be adopted by professionals and amateurs alike.

Hopefully, it will be this understanding of the importance of an audience's participatory, rather than passive, role in receiving the work that will steer you safely away from self-indulgence and introspection. If it is your intention to study dramatic texts academically then academic truth may be your guiding light, and your responsibilities will be only to the written word. However, if you are a theatre practitioner, working upon drama for the practical intent of its interpretation, then the audience must be your ultimate master and the faithful representation of the playwright's toil your ultimate inspiration and goal.

Another important factor is how an audience may react to the very nature of interpretation. Depending upon the work in question, they may have very strong personal preconceptions as to how a play should be performed and to what extent its interpretation should be predetermined.

You can look again to Shakespearian texts as a prime and pertinent example of this. While many people view the plays as magnificently 'open books' with regard to their treatment, others see them as sacred objects to be presented in terms of traditionalism. Ironically, the root of this traditionalism is often difficult to identify, as the plays cover many different periods of history, employ a great deal of dramatic licence in their original conception and were never performed in costume and style pertinent to their setting when originally performed anyway. You will certainly be aware of the reluctance many people have to accept 'modern dress' productions of Shakespearian plays but, rather than dismiss this as an ignorant misunderstanding of the role of the production and to the sanctity of the text, you should view this type of comment as a pointer to the importance of interpretation and how it can be misconstrued.

Very often, when railing against what an audience sees as 'messing about' with Shakespeare, it is the nature and integrity of interpretation that is really being questioned rather than its necessity. It is rare that a high quality and honestly conceived production is criticized for its interpretational intentions, but a poorly conceived and dishonest attempt will be roundly pilloried as being almost blasphemous. It is not the job of the audience to realize that any play needs to be interpreted at all – they need not be aware of your role beyond that of simple storyteller. However, it is your job to realize that interpretation is vital and in order not to be sanctioned for the very execution of your job you need to ensure that all of your analysis and research stands up to scrutiny and makes a case for itself that can be answered in relation to the actual integrity and intentions of the text.

In short, interpretation must warrant its existence. It is not given a free place in the process of dramatic art but is required to earn it. In order to ensure this practically, you must endeavour always to be honest and truthful to the text and the author's intentions as you perceive them. Do not impose yourself upon the text; rather offer up your skills in humble partnership. A production may aim to be extraordinary, ground-breaking, innovative, inspired and, even, revolutionary, but if it is not rooted in textual truth it will fail in all of this and be viewed as shallow and gimmicky. As you progress with this you will be surprised at just how wide and far-reaching your interpretations may be, but you must also learn to recognize and accept what they cannot be and where your own inspiration must give way to truth.

Be aware, too, that an audience member utilizes his or her feelings and emotions in respect of the drama just as much as you and the playwright. The difference is that their role is unplanned, unpredicted and instant; their involvement can be immediate and total. Remember this and respect it. If the play and your work are good they should 'do' something to the audience: that is change the individual in some, maybe only small, way and mark the drama as a significant experience in the life of that person. You should not aim to give your audiences an easy ride, but neither forget that they are part of the process and not just the recipients of it. As you work, be always mindful of what you might be doing to your patrons, why you are doing it and whether its relevance

23

is worthy of the commitment and energy that you hope they will contribute in their receiving of the work.

The Way Ahead

Having now established firmly in your mind the importance of the work you are to undertake and your place within the unique three-way artistic experience of drama, you are ready to move forward with confidence. Your journey of discovery will blend your ability to discover tangible backgrounds to the texts you are to study with an aptitude to apply your own thoughts, ideas and experiences to the work. You will require a love of drama, and an enquiring and open mind. Paradoxically, although research and analysis may sound an academic and dusty process, when applied to drama it becomes the opposite; for drama is probably as close to broadly accessible living

Performance must affect the audience.

art as you can reasonably get, and its study requires a total engagement in life and the complexities of the human experience. This is no job for someone who sits on the sidelines of the world and observes. A painter may retire and withdraw from the world to paint; a drama practitioner can afford no such luxury, for they must always be at the forefront of life, ready to relish the gift of life at every opportunity. To be a good interpreter of dramatic art you must have your feet planted firmly on the 'shop floor'.

Finally, be brave enough to do your work diligently and honestly and then hand it freely to an audience for it to play its part. There will be many times when your efforts are rewarded, by some, with disinterest or even disdain. Do not let this overly concern you; take the rough with the smooth, do your best and have faith in the three-way process of drama. The ultimate rewards will be many and your positive results will easily outweigh the negative.

2 PICKING UP THE PLAY

A FIRST STEP

The process of researching, analysing and interpreting text begins with the simple act of reading through the play for the first time. From the outset there are two possible scenarios: that you know the play, have read or seen it before, or that you are approaching it for the very first time. Neither of these is necessarily a particular advantage or, indeed, disadvantage; the important thing is to open the book with an equally open mind.

If you come to the text with a ready-made knowledge of it, to whatever degree, do so positively for this knowledge is work already 'banked' and will be of great use to you. However, remind yourself that there is always more to learn and, more importantly, your perception, understanding and even your opinion of the play is a fluid thing and can change. Make sure that you do not allow familiarity to blind you to new and vibrant revelations that await your work upon the text on this occasion. It is one of the great joys of art when one begins to see it in a 'new light', but this will not happen if you have strait-jacketed yourself with past reactions to it.

Also be wary of predetermining a reaction to a play you have not personally encountered before, based upon the opinions of others, the particular genre or the reputation of the playwright. Nothing blocks the creative process more than a prejudicial view of your subject matter.

PERSONAL VIEWPOINTS

One of your first reactions to the play is very likely to be a feeling of how much you like or, conversely, dislike it. Hopefully, this opinion will not be 'set in stone' but first impressions are certainly relevant and important. There are two main determining factors at work here: one is the quality of the writing and the other is the thematic approach or philosophy of the work. The first of these you can do very little about, save for realizing that the amount of useful interpretation that you can draw out of a play will inevitably be dependent to a large extent upon its quality. The second is much more relevant. You may find yourself very much in tune with the playwright's view, or even choice, of subject matter; on the other hand, you may equally be opposed to it or even alienated by it. Neither of these extremes is particularly healthy and ideally your reaction will be to find middle ground with a positive appreciation of the arguments for and against the author's standpoint; or, in a totally ideal world, an empathy for the playwright's own balanced view of the subject. This may well be the case if the theme of the play is broad and encompasses open reflection on the human condition. However, it is less likely to be the case if the theme is strongly issue-based and the play aims to make a particular point or points in political, religious or philosophical terms.

However, do not be afraid of a polarized reaction, if you have one, because to play your part in the three-way interpretation process (as already discussed in Chapter 1) your contribution must be a 'human' one and to be human to take a view. The important thing is to utilize the advantages of a strong personal reaction and to negate the disadvantages. In order to do this you must examine what these advantages and disadvantages are in the context of both a positive and negative 'first impression' of the author's theme.

Become a Critic

In order to develop your unique personal viewpoint of the work you undertake as either (or both) an actor or director, but to develop it in a constructive, non-judgemental unprejudiced way, it is helpful to get into a habit of evaluating everything that you come across in your daily life that is in any way artistic or creative. This constant practice will sharpen your instinctive response of balanced opinion. The following are just a few examples of subject matter.

- When you are reading a newspaper, consider your opinion not just of the journalist's views but also of their writing style.
- Consider the attributes of the photographs you see in magazines and note their merits in terms of composition and flair.
- Evaluate the performances of actors that you see on television. However, do not be too unkind as they are your 'brothers and sisters'. Think, too, about the different shots and camera angles in a television drama and how effective they are. This can often be taken for granted but is a fascinating area to consider.
- When you hear a tune or song that you like or don't like, attempt to reason why this is so – try to hum the melody and improve upon it by adding notes and changes of tempo so that you become very aware of its construction.
- Look closely and smell every flower you encounter and savour its effect upon you.

IDENTIFYING AREAS OF RESEARCH

Many theatre practitioners have very good intentions about the amount and quality of preparatory work that they intend to devote to a new project, but let the time slip and eventually find themselves entering the rehearsal period with few, if any of their worthy ambitions fulfilled. It is certainly more difficult for directors to make this mistake, as it is particularly costly for them when they meet their cast on the first day of rehearsal woefully unprepared, but actors, who can perhaps escape detection more easily, are often guilty of inadequate preparation.

However, as you are reading this book, it can be confidently assumed that you do not wish to replicate this type of mistake.

The key to avoiding this pitfall is to decide and list, from the outset of receiving the script, the exact nature of the research work that will be needed prior to rehearsals starting. Later, in another chapter, you will find a breakdown of some of the main types of dramatic work from different periods and suggestions as to the varying type of research they may require. Use this to help you make your list but remember, too, that selecting research criteria is not only about what others may perceive to be the academic requirements at hand but also how you, as the practitioner – the person who actually has to bring the piece to exciting and stimulating life – identify your own needs in terms of preparation. These will be based upon your own areas of weaknesses of knowledge and, much more importantly, the information and support you need to enable your particular and unique contribution to the play. In the same way as your artistic endeavours upon a piece will always be different and individual to others (for such is the beauty of art), so will your research be equally individualistic and particular as you structure it to your thoughts and intentions regarding the play.

Remember that all of the research that you will undertake, on any particular project, should be designed and dedicated to helping you interpret the play: you are working for yourself and your labours must be angled towards making you a better theatre practitioner in every sense. Your work will be judged at its face value – your performance or the quality of a production you have directed. No audience member will be aware of the amount or type of research you have done but they will be very much aware of the results of it, so make sure that it suits your purpose.

IDENTIFYING AREAS OF ANALYSIS

The first reading of a script upon which you are to work should be an incredibly exciting experience for you: for this is the time when the possibilities for the production should seem vast and the practical difficulties (yet to be encountered) insignificant. The thrill of possibilities to come and opportunities to be explored will be palpable. This feeling should not only manifest itself when faced with artistically challenging works but also when squaring up to more mundane, straightforward and, perhaps, less well-written plays, for the anticipatory buzz can be just as acute when contemplating the task of bringing a flat, two-dimensional character to rounded, three-dimensional life as when savouring the opportunity of liberating great and intellectually stimulating themes from the pages of a masterpiece.

Much of this initial excitement will be the result of the potential analysis to come. The prospects of interpreting character, making sense of a theme, exploring a personal response to the subject matter, investigating historical background and social context will all be enticing in the extreme. If this is not the case then there is something wrong, as the desire to interpret should be the theatre practitioner's first and instinctive response to all drama, whatever its type.

Thus, then, the first reading will provide a chance to savour these delights to come. While it is possible to provisionally list the various research tasks that may lie ahead for study, it is not really possible to be quite so exact in terms of analytical possibilities. This will be more a case of giving rein to your sensitivity, opening your mind and letting the play speak to you as directly as possible upon this first encounter. You should allow (but not force) your thoughts and feelings to engage with the subject matter and to begin to make some

The Analytical Habit

In life it is very easy to get into the habit of taking things for granted and accepting them at face value. However, this is an adult foible and children tend to take the opposite approach. A child will question everything, want to know how everything works and why and generally consider everything in relation to themselves and how they are affected by it all. A good theatre practitioner will start to view the world through the eyes of a child again; to see the obvious rather than being blind to it and not be afraid to ask awkward questions in order to find relevant answers.

This habit of analysing life as you encounter it can take many forms and degrees, ranging from considering why a machine works in a particular way, dwelling upon how a goldfish views the world outside its bowl and wrestling with the thorny problem of the meaning of life itself.

A habitually enquiring and analysing mind will make for instinctive and thoughtful work when studying text.

preliminary impressions of your reaction to it (although not too dramatically at this stage). You should identify for later areas that you might explore yourself and in discussion with others, and commence to relish the prospect for further study and interpretation. The main job here is to begin to formulate your ideas (avoiding prejudice) and to get a feel for the analysis to come.

STARTING TO HEAR YOUR 'VOICE'

It is quite obvious that the best approach to interpreting drama, whether performing or directing it, is to build as slowly and carefully as possible, avoiding the temptation to leap to conclusions and make decisions that may become entrenched. The first reading of a script is the best opportunity you will have to take this approach. However, it is inevitable that, being only human, you will automatically start to hear your 'voice' in the play. Your 'voice' in this context means not only the actual sounds you make – the kind of voice you will use for the character – but your whole reading of the part; that is, your look, gait, manner, movement and attitude to the part. If you are a director, your 'voice' means the unique personal interpretation you will place upon the play – what you will have to 'say' about it.

Wary of the pitfalls of instantly interpreting a text and thus strait-jacketing yourself at such an early stage, you may very well panic when hearing this 'voice' and attempt to ignore or suppress it. This will only make matters worse. As already said, it is inevitable that you will hear it as your response to a play, and your anticipation of your work upon it will be quite instinctive, which is only right and proper. So the best course of action is to accept the 'voice' and treat its manifestation positively but with a dose of caution. If viewed in the right way, this reaction to a first reading can be extremely helpful.

In fact, rather than try to diminish the 'voice', encourage it and let it have its free rein. Imagine yourself with many pots of paint of bright and varying colours. Then imagine that your first reading is akin to painting with these colours upon a vast canvas, with a very large brush and with complete abandon and little regard to technique or even control. You know that later you will be able to repaint the picture with refined brushstrokes and thinner, more delicate brushes but, for the time being, you are uninhibitedly experimenting with the myriad of possibilities that the paint offers and the wide variety of painting skills that you are able to use in an ideal situation.

If you consider the hearing of your 'voice' in this way it will no longer seem to be a limiting or confining thing but an opportunity to examine all possibilities of potential – the great array of devices and skills that you can bring to the project – prior to the more arduous task of selecting, refining and employing these thoughtfully and with discernment. In addition, this exaggerated and unfettered encouragement of the 'voice' will, in its absurdity of scale, not be restricting or encumbering for the future but rather act as a wonderfully uncompromising and liberating preview of possibilities – a snapshot of a wide and generous palate!

You may very well find the first communal read-through with the cast at the beginning of rehearsals equally useful for exactly the same reasons. Therefore, if you are directing, try to have such a read-through prior to starting work on the play, provided time allows this luxury. The exercise can pay dividends and be well worth the time invested.

OPPOSITE: Encourage your 'voice'.

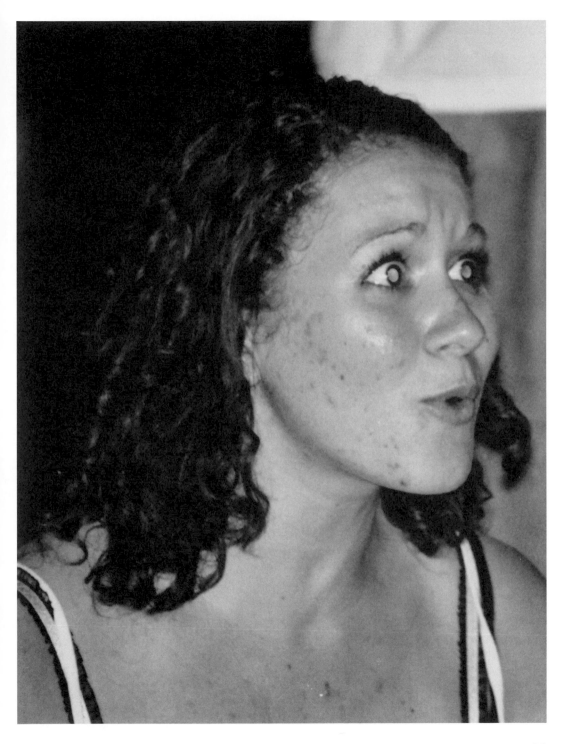

PRE-RESEARCH RESEARCH

While the process of research should be seen as something to be looked forward to and enjoyed, and therefore not to be rushed or in any sense be got out of the way, there are one or two mundane and irksome matters that can be dealt with during the first reading of a script in order to clear the way for the more important elements of research to be undertaken later.

These are the matters of basic meaning and pronunciation. Have a dictionary (one that includes phonetic spellings will be best) by your side as you read the play and make sure that you identify those things that you don't understand. Some of these may be naturally complex in relation to the subject matter of the work and should be left for future investigation, but other more straightforward meanings of words that you have not encountered before, or of which you have simply never known the exact meaning, should be dealt with immediately so as not to hamper you with triviality later on.

You should also remember that before long you will be reading the script out loud for the first time in front of others. You will need to be confident in your speaking and knowledge of the words and phrases. Working upon a text, both by yourself and with others, is an arduous (if fulfilling) process and one to be commenced with as clear and uncomplicated a view of the task and source material as possible.

DON'T BE CRITICAL OF THE PLAY

It is hoped that much, if not most, of the plays upon which you work will be of a high and enriching standard. However, it would be naive to think that this will always be the case and it is reasonably certain that you will be presented with some poor quality work from time to time.

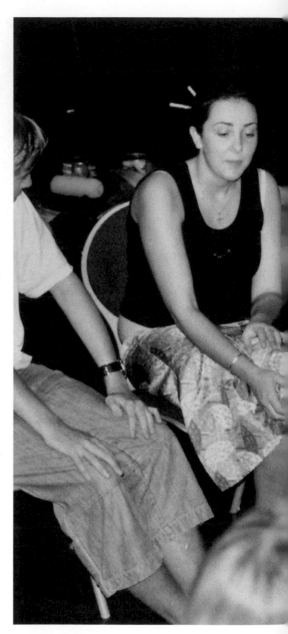

It has already been established that such plays can be just as challenging, in their way, as their more challenging stable mates but, as a sensitive artist, you will be well aware of the difference and very able to make the distinction.

It will not be necessary for you to pretend that an indifferent play is good or even that a bad one is acceptable, but it is wise not to be too critical in your condemnation as this negativity is likely to infect and poison your approach.

Be confident in your opinion of the play.

Try, if you can, to be positive about even the most inadequate of work and look for the pluses rather than the minuses. Remember that most bad plays will possess some redeeming features. It is your job to look for these and accentuate them with your valuable contributions. There is nothing wrong in taking this confident attitude, but you should avoid being patronizing or condemnatory, even in the privacy of your own mind: it will make you complacent and stifle your creativity. Drama is not an easy venture for any of its participants; if it were it would not be worth doing in the first place. It is just as humanly possible for an author to write a bad play as it is for an actor to give a bad performance or a director to construct a bad production.

Therefore, work with the playwright positively with the intention of making every element of the production, and every person's contribution to it, shine as much as possible. A sympathetic and non-critical outlook may not be as much fun as the short-term confidence fillip of dwelling upon a colleague's weaknesses (for a playwright is your colleague even though you may not know them), but generally 'one reaps what one sows' and resistance to overt criticism will be far more sustaining and helpful to you in the long term.

It is very possible in some instances that you know the author of the play that you are to work upon; they may even be a good friend. This is obviously a time when lack of criticism and plenty of honest, positive thinking (and tact) will be particularly wise.

With all of this in mind, you are now ready to move further on into the delight of understanding text.

Be positive in your work.

3 THE NEED TO RESEARCH AND ANALYSE

NEED INDEED

Many people believe that acting and drama are not intellectual disciplines. Often, in the world of education, it will be assumed that a pupil or student who is ill-disposed to academic work (either through lack of ability or willingness of application) will do well (and perhaps even flourish) in the world of the dramatic arts, giving them a chance to express themselves without the rigours of constructive thought, concentration and study.

Unfortunately, this is not generally true. Certainly, drama may inspire, motivate and galvanize an individual who previously had not found (or sought) sufficient mental stimulus and thus this individual may suddenly 'find their legs' and begin to truly fulfil their potential both as an actor (or director) and as a human being. However, those without any desire or ability to utilize and apply intellect will struggle as much as in any other subject.

This is most definitely not to say that theatre practitioners need to be geniuses or have even above normal cleverness, but some degree of effective mental ability is needed if drama is to rise above the basics of mere 'play' and be practised as an art form and craft. All that *is needed* in this regard is an average education and average intelligence, but *it is needed* in order to research and analyse. This book, by its very existence, establishes the vital importance of both of these factors and to do either effectively requires some, if not necessarily a vast amount of, mental agility and discipline.

EDUCATION

An average education is required by the theatre practitioner in order to identify the various areas of research and analysis required and to have some reference points to guide them. Many plays deal with very specific historical and political events and movements and thus require particular and complex research in order to understand their context and liberate them successfully from the page. In such cases you will be at a disadvantage if you are starting from scratch: a general understanding and some (if sketchy) background knowledge will furnish you with a starting point and system of reference along the way. Research without analysis is useless (utilization of knowledge needs an ability to interpret and understand it personally) and an actor or director will not be able to process information effectively if they find themselves immersed in subject matter of which they have no knowledge or understanding, albeit perfunctory.

Even a vague idea of what the subject is about, its context and relevance, will give the theatre practitioner easier access to its research. Education breeds education and analysis breeds analysis. That is to say that knowledge and its interpretation will lead to and facilitate further knowledge and interpretation; it is a cumulative process gathering pace and energy as pieces of a jigsaw are located and fitted together. So a lively and inquiring mind that has a reasonable knowledge of the world and its secrets will be ready and able to begin the process while a closed, inactive and uninformed mind will struggle to get beyond first base.

However, it is important to remember that, for your purposes, education is not necessarily that of academia. An average education can be possessed by anyone, no matter what his or her formal education may be. The key here is true open-mindedness, inquisitiveness, interest in the world and love of knowledge for its own sake. A good theatre practitioner should read as much as possible and should endeavour to develop an eclectic taste in books. They should travel widely and immerse themselves in as wide and diverse a mix of cultural, artistic experiences as possible. If you are serious about developing your ability to research, analyse and interpret texts (and indeed to be a good theatre practitioner), you must visit art galleries, museums, theatres and libraries regularly. Try to be interested in as much as possible, for this will provide you with the education you need as well as the energy and enthusiasm to apply it.

INTELLIGENCE

An average intelligence is required in order to not only gather the information but to process it. However, in a sense, the word intelligence is somewhat misleading: it is intellect that is really important for your purposes. Intellect is the ability to use intelligence, to apply it and make the most of it as a tool and enabler. An actor or director does not need to be a 'brain box' in any respect, but they do need that average intellect that will allow them to play their part in the 'three-way process': they will need to respect the work, to understand its themes, to appreciate its qualities, to identify its shortcomings, to absorb its knowledge, to acquire more knowledge associated with it and (most importantly) to be able to find and utilize their own personal reaction to the work in parts and as a whole.

Thus it is important that you aim to stretch your mind intellectually as much as you can. Be quick to formulate opinions about things and be prepared to defend your position; engage in debate and discussion at every opportunity; play chess and do cross-

An intelligent approach is key.

words – anything that will sharpen your brain.

An average education and intelligence (intellect) may be no problem for you as you may be well beyond and above both. However, if not, it is very possible that both are within your reach and you should apply yourself diligently to that end.

A dull, slow, uninterested, unresponsive, lazy, closed mind will never be successful at maths, geography, history, art or any other subject, including drama, despite the beliefs of ill-informed and patronizing people who think otherwise.

An Example of the Need to Research and Analyse

An eminent and respected acting tutor had a student who, despite an obvious talent and ability for acting, struggled to bring her characters to life or to fully engage with them. She was lazy and did the minimum of work, believing that she could 'act' and that, therefore, everything would fall into place and she would happily reap success with very little intellectual effort on her part at all. However, her exam results were poor. She failed miserably to convince her examiners that she had seriously studied the plays that her pieces (speeches prepared for the exam) were taken from and the pieces themselves were lacking in life, commitment and integrity.

Her teacher persevered, continually entreating her to work harder, to study more and to simply think about the plays and the playwrights. Surprised and discouraged by her poor results she gradually began to realize her failings and started to apply herself more diligently to her studies. For her next examination, and having to portray the character of Nina in a speech from *The Seagull* by Anton Chekhov, she began, not only to research

(reading the play, other plays by the same author, background study of the playwright, historical and social scrutiny and so on), but she allowed this research to prompt her into thinking about the play in an appreciative and analytical way. On the day of her exam and while in the waiting room prior to her appointed time she got into a conversation about the play with another student who was studying the same part. As both had been working hard on the text the discussion flowed and, because this particular student had now a background of research and analysis to her work (albeit quite basic), she found herself formulating an extremely interesting and progressive theory about the character and, more particularly, the play.

She recognized a parallel between the preoccupation of *The Seagull*'s plot and Chekhov's own unique place in world drama at the time of his writings: on the one hand, there was the conflict between old-fashioned and dated concepts of theatre and new more issue-driven, down-to-earth and socially recognizable drama, and on the other, Chekhov's revolutionary mission to produce work of more social relevance and psychological insight and exploration than theatre had known in previous years.

The substance and angle of her discussion was open to argument and debate but she was able to defend it and, more importantly, it was an insight that had sprung uniquely from her – the pure result of research and analysis. Not only did she impress the examiner with her illuminations upon this subject but her new and enhanced understanding of the text brought new life, depth and emotional connection to her performance when she presented the speech. Most significant of all, she was truly surprised (and delighted) that her modest and comparatively undemanding efforts had resulted in yielding such rich and productive rewards.

IDENTIFYING THE MAJOR AREAS OF RESEARCH

Research must precede analysis. Obviously each and every play that you encounter will have its own particular (perhaps even peculiar) requirements in terms of the research needed. One of the most exciting things about drama is the ever diversifying journey of discovery and enlightenment that is to be encountered in every new script that you work upon. Both old and new writing contains a wealth of fascination and bedazzlement – rich seams of precious material just waiting to be mined and utilized by you. The range of knowledge, subject matter and philosophical insight that you will be presented with will be large and widely encompassing. It is indeed the strength of drama (as an artistic form) that its boundaries of content and experience are no more restricted than those of life itself.

However, there are certainly some broad identifiable areas that will help you to concentrate your mind upon the particular necessities of research required. Into these basic headings the plethora of theatrical ideas, strewn amongst the rich diversity of plays on offer, can be placed not so as to confine them but to help you to focus upon the particular areas of research that all may engage you in. There follow some very basic and broad areas of research that will, hopefully, help you to perceive and clarify your task in unravelling the content of a play. Most plays will contain research opportunities in at least one (but in many cases, each) of these basic areas.

All of your work, research and analysis must inevitably lead you to an understanding of 'character' and the ability to breathe credible life into a fictitious persona. Thus research into 'character' and the areas of psychological analysis should be seen as a culmination of the process of research rather than a particular topic of it (a pulling together of research and

analysis into a living whole). This is therefore dealt with in detail in a separate chapter.

HISTORICAL

It is essential to have as thorough and detailed a knowledge and, more importantly, understanding of the historical period in which the play is set as possible. This will not apply if it is entirely contemporary, but even if the story takes place in the relatively recent past, thorough research of the period should be undertaken, although, in these cases, the research may be more a process of regenerating memory rather than an academic exercise.

Remember that you are in the business of bringing characters to life within the landscape of the drama. Therefore the emphasis of your research should be placed firmly upon the way in which an historical period affected people and their institutions. For instance, a detailed knowledge of politics in the nineteenth century is useless unless it is accompanied by an understanding of its relevance to the lives of the populace at the time. Then again, an understanding of this based upon one particular class or section of society is of greater use if you also possess a broad overview. In the same way, researching, say, the social and sexual morality of the period must include its differing effects upon various types of people, but must also be firmly angled towards the characters in the play and how and in what ways they are influenced by it.

The starting point for any historical research must be to identify the period in which the play is actually set. This may seem like a ridiculously obvious statement but it is utterly surprising how many actors do not possess this information, even after they have been working upon the text for some time. Often they feel that it is

OPPOSITE: History is a main area of research.

enough to have a vague impression of the historical setting, knowing that it takes place in the past and having a very rough notion of how far back this is. It is impossible for such an actor to be seriously studying the play and their character, or to be rehearsing effectively beyond merely 'practising' an arbitrary rendition of the lines: for without knowing when a play is set one cannot begin to acquire an understanding of that period and how it will influence the actions, opinions, motivations, prejudices, aspirations, vulnerabilities, interactions and capabilities (to name but a few) of its characters.

Finding out the period of the play will not be difficult, as it will usually be stated at the front of the script or in the early stage directions within the text. This adds even more incredulity to the fact that actors may be unaware of this information long after they have started work on the play – but it does happen.

Having established the time in which the play is set, the actual researching into this period need not be too arduous, provided it is relevant. If you are directing you may certainly wish to study considerably and widely, and this is advisable as part of your preparation before rehearsals start. If you are acting in the production it will not do you any harm at all to be just as thorough, again focusing the bulk of this work prior to rehearsals if you possibly can. However, the most important factor to be considered here is that quality is very much more beneficial than quantity. It is essential that you target your research into areas that are relevant to the play.

These are likely to be the areas that deal most directly with the situations and actions of the characters, but to identify these more specifically it is a good plan for an actor to start in exactly the same way as they should approach all areas of research and analytical development generally; you should ask yourself some basic questions. Each of these questions will be asked in terms of a particular 'factor' of research, the

A Warning about Stage Directions

It must not be forgotten that stage directions can be very helpful in terms of research and the analysis of character and text, simply by fact of the information that they contain. However, be careful, as some are of more use than others. It is important to ascertain if these directions come directly from the playwright or whether their origin is from a previous production of the play. Obviously, description and views from the author are invaluable (although even they should only be seen as a starting point for your own research and eventual interpretation), but 'second-hand' information is less useful and must be treated with discrimination; it may well be a helpful chance for you to utilize the work of others but it may also be misleading. Sometimes stage directions have been lifted directly from a stage management script of the original production of the play and, as such, may not be relevant to the personal interpretation of your own version of the work at all.

'factor' that you are presently examining being the historical period.

- How does this factor affect the living conditions of the characters in the play?
- How does this factor affect the physical practicalities of their daily lives – housing, clothing, diet, and so on?
- How does this factor affect the behaviour of the characters?
- How does this factor influence the choices they make?
- How does this factor affect their personalities?
- How does this factor affect their opportunities and constraints?

- How does this factor affect their outlook on life?
- How does this factor affect the tensions and conflicts within the play

Directors will most certainly ask the same questions but, obviously, far more in terms of a wider perspective, an equally balanced regard to all of the characters, and perhaps with a greater emphasis early upon how the answers to these questions affect the interaction between characters – knowledge that actors will discover naturally later in the process of rehearsals.

Remember that all 'factors' of research will interlink (historical period cannot be divorced from geographical location, for instance).

In order to observe how these questions can lead to specific areas of rewarding historical research (as they can in all other areas), it is always helpful to look at them in the context of examples from particular plays. In the comedy play *Hobson's Choice* by Harold Brighouse, set in 1880s Salford in Lancashire, the central character, Maggie, is a prime example of how historical period formulates and shapes character and motivation. This is, in many ways, an underrated play. It is often seen as dated and categorized as a 'popular' comedy, aimed firmly at entertaining its audience in an escapist and light-hearted manner. However, while it is certainly this, it also has a lot more to offer in terms of an examination of human frailties, personal aspirations, loyalty

Target your research.

and the conflicts of family life. As with so many good plays it presents a compelling insight into the 'human condition' within the context of its plot and setting.

Maggie is an extremely strong person, effectively in charge of her father's boot-making business; she is full of confidence and guile and extremely adept at manipulating those around her, including her stubborn and curmudgeonly father. She is forthright in manner and prides herself in controlling every situation and winning every battle. Coupled with this, she is extremely practical and can organize herself and others with military precision.

While a historical understanding of Victorian society may lead you to be surprised at such characteristics in a female character, it may also enable you to understand it. Maggie has been forced by circumstance to compete in a man's world at a time when women were very much supposed to be submissive and sometimes servile. She cannot afford to let anyone or anything get the better of her, and her experience of needing to manage a business that her father would ruin left to his own devices, and needing to do so against the intransigent perception of the society she lived in of a woman's 'proper' place and mode of behaviour, has forced her to either sink or swim. The fact that she has been able to very much 'swim' is, of course, due to how various facets of her personality have reacted to the shaping of external influences, but nonetheless these external influences have doubtless been responsible for the manner in which the raw ingredients of her character have melded into such a strong and resilient person.

Your research can lead you to think about these historically based external influences in quite specific ways. For instance, Maggie will have had to deal with representatives trying to sell her materials and stock at inflated prices, men who would believe her, as a woman in an extremely unusual position for the times, to be easy prey and ripe for 'conning'. In order to combat this, and save her father's business from ruin, she would have needed to play these men at their own game, put her femininity to one side, and deal with them as a man would do in her society. Thus, she has become strong, not through choice, but through necessity.

Of course, a woman playing Maggie today will not be devoid of the experiences of the character she is playing, many women are still forced to compete in a world traditionally still dominated by men. However, although this may be seen as an advantage for the actor's understanding of the part, it could also be a disadvantage, in that the actor may underestimate the effect upon her character by failing to appreciate the greater degree of pressure that the attitudes of that particular period would exert upon her. It is here where historical research becomes vital.

Continuing with the particular example, it is not enough to assume a particular social attitude and expect that to inform an understanding of a character's personality. Social attitudes can be universal and, to some extent, timeless. What is required is detailed research into the practical manifestations of that social attitude, for when applying all of the questions, previously mentioned, you must do so in terms of specifics. These specifics can be manifold and will cross with other areas of research. The types of roles normally expected of women may be looked at – not just the obvious ones within the home, but also the kind of jobs that women might aspire to outside. Costume is another important factor, as the kind of attire worn by an individual is firmly linked to an appreciation of their place in society and the philosophies to which they may be expected (or indeed want) to conform.

Still with the same example, it is not specific enough for you to know the 'kind' of attitudes and pressures experienced by women of the period; you must know the ways in which these manifest themselves. At what age was a woman supposed to marry? – a very pertinent question in the case of *Hobson's Choice* as Maggie is considered to be very much 'on the shelf' and uses her practical outlook and capabilities to ensnare a husband. What kind of men were women of a particular position and class expected to marry? Maggie's choice of the bootmaker, Willy Mossop, is thought highly inappropriate for her, but she knows differently. How were women supposed to conduct themselves in terms of, not only dress, but posture and movement? How were they supposed to speak? When and in what context?

It is only when you are able to approach your research in terms of specifics and detail that you will be able to begin to ask (and answer) the 'eight questions' detailed earlier with any kind of success.

It should be stressed again, that any one area of research (such as, in this case, historical) cannot be applied unilaterally and must be seen as a building block towards an understanding of the play and its characters. The divine spark; the core of originality; the particular and fascinating constitution of 'soul' that every character worth playing possesses, is found through a conglomerate of analysis and, paradoxically, it is these precious factors of personality that react with particular research criteria (such as 'historical') to determine the given characteristics and associated motivations of the particular character.

By way of perfect example, in *Hobson's Choice*, Maggie's sisters, Alice and

Research and analysis equal character.

41

Vicky, are characteristically diametrically opposite to her. They are vane, conceited, lazy, appreciative of their perceived position of 'weak females' and preoccupied with materialism, frivolity and marriage to 'the right man'. However, it is the very same factors of historical research and its analysis that can bring the actors playing them to an understanding of 'how' they have come to be so and 'why' they act as they do. In their case, the pressures and preoccupations of the play's historical setting have moulded them into the beings that they are. It is simply their complacency to these influences and Maggie's active antagonism to them that so vividly divides them as siblings. The reasons for these conflicting choices of reaction can be found both in the unifying of all strands of research and in the particular analysis of 'character' (which you will look at in a later chapter), but the integrity of the particular research applied to each character remains true and its relevance invaluable to directors and actors alike.

PHILOSOPHICAL, POLITICAL AND RELIGIOUS BACKGROUND

This is a very important area of research and most good plays (and also some poor ones) will contain at least some element of philosophical, political or (and) religious content and intent. Indeed, some plays will be strongly founded on one or more of these, with their whole agenda focused upon an exploration of a particular issue or issues.

A play of this nature is likely to place its factual and metaphorical content within a framework pertinent to its theme: it may be set within a particular political landscape or refer heavily to a strand of philosophical theory or religious tract.

It is in this area that you are most likely to encounter the greatest degree of personal

To 'Know' is not to 'Understand'

It must be noted that a keyword often applied to the results of research is 'understanding'. This is vitally important, for mere knowledge, in terms of the academic 'fact and figures' of research, is inadequate to the task in hand. Actors and directors are not involved in an essentially academic pursuit – they are concerned not with incontrovertible, black and white information but with the much less definable process of applying that information to the essentially artistic job of bringing fictitious characters and situations (that exist, at the outset, only in terms of dry words on an inanimate page) to realistic, believable, spontaneous and colourful life upon the stage.

Therefore, it is of little use if research and analysis simply lead a theatre practitioner to know why people in the play are as they are and behave as they do. It is not until they can understand and truly feel these things that they are able to turn academic appreciation into practical application. It is simply not enough just to know the details; the details must be made personal and relevant to the work in order to find a living relevance for everything that happens in the play, and to validate and illuminate the playwright's reasons for creating it.

reaction. In remembering that this particular aspect of a play will, by its very nature, instigate a strong response from its audience, be aware also that it will so with you as the practitioner. This is a wholly positive factor: after all, it is to be expected, indeed desired, that a good play will engender feelings and opinions in those who watch it – this is part of the purpose of drama. By the same token, it essential to the process of the theatrical venture (especially in terms of the three-way contributory process) that you, too, are moved, stimulated and motivated by such themes within the work.

However, beware – for there are pitfalls to be avoided here, especially in the area of your research. You may be very much in sympathy with the political, religious or philosophical theme of the play. It may well be that this is the very reason you have become involved with the project or, at least, part of its attraction. While this, again, is certainly advantageous, there is an obvious risk that you might lack a sufficient degree of balance and objectivity. It is important not to lose sight of the fact that good drama, whatever its theme, must also contain a broad and inclusive view of the human condition and not just communicate a 'message' in dramatic form. In other words, it must not just 'hammer' its point but make it poetically and dramatically in the context of the overall situation of its characters and their strengths, frailties and perceptions. It is very easy, both as a director and as an actor to tip this balance and push the play towards preaching to its audience if you are overenthusiastic and, particularly, evangelistic in your approach. Thus, at the researching stage, be sure to remain cool, calm and objective as you gather, process and assimilate the facts, together with your understanding and interpretation of them.

There is equal danger in the opposite reaction and opinion of a political, religious or philosophical theme. A theatre practitioner is not always afforded the luxury of being able to choose the plays upon which they work. You may find yourself totally or, at best, partly opposed to the theme and intentions of the script. Indeed, in some cases this reaction may be extreme and forceful. There is nothing essentially wrong with this: if actors and directors are to take a professional attitude to their work and, in many cases, earn their living from it, then an ability to tackle subjects that are to a greater or lesser degree alien to their own

'idea of the world' is not only expedient but also fundamentally desirable and productive.

However, as before, the correct approach to work of this nature is all-important. In such circumstances you must place yourself somewhat in the position of 'devil's advocate': you must to a degree suspend your own ideas and opinions (and, perhaps, prejudices) and approach the work with an open mind. On the other hand, do not try to ignore, forget or (worst of all) bury your own reactions to the play, for this could be disastrous – as in life generally, anything that is buried has a habit of unexpectedly and violently resurfacing with often disagreeable and uncontrollable results. The best way to proceed is to put yourself into the mind of the playwright. Try to understand their world, appreciate their views, experiences and intentions for the work, while, at the same time, ensuring that you do not deny your own opinions and appreciations of their themes (however anti they may be). Thus you will bring yourself and your ideas to the work as a participating and constructive partner, with valued and useful reactions but not with condemnation and reproach.

It is important that you understand that, in a situation where you are not in sympathy with the tenets of the play, you must respectfully and honestly try to approach the work from the author's point of view without ignoring or sidelining your own. In doing this, you will hopefully find points of reference and areas of mutual empathy that will allow you to do research and interpret the work productively and with integrity even though you may not personally advocate its themes and purposes. This means finding a way to champion the playwright's work from within yourself and not to change, corrupt or adapt it to suit your own purposes or preconceptions. You must not compromise the playwright or yourself, for to do so would be to denigrate the work and destroy the unique relationship between author, practitioner and audience.

This ideal is not as difficult to achieve as it may sound. All good drama, however committed it may be to progressing a particular idea or philosophy, should contain a broad enough range of ideas, angles and balanced insights to enable you to find common ground and aspects of the theme, the truth of which you can appreciate, even if you cannot necessarily agree with them. Very often it is possible to understand a 'truth' in general terms even if it is not 'true' to your own particular creed or code. Embracing these 'truths' and having respect for the playwright's point of view (without pandering to it) should enable you to find a route forwards into understanding and faithfully interpreting the play.

Therefore, as you start and continue to research keep all of this very firmly in your mind. Research is, of course, the foundation of all that will follow in terms of interpretation and application, so it should be sound, balanced and constructive from the outset.

An extremely pertinent example of this point can be found and examined in the play *Masterpieces* by Sarah Daniels. Its topic and viewpoint is not only relevant to the subject of political themes (socio-political in this case) but presents how an antipathy towards a play can be instinctive and, as such, can

Drama 'pulls no punches'.

blind a practitioner to its worth, not to say brilliance.

Broadly speaking, *Masterpieces* is a play that deals with the brutal dehumanizing effects of pornography, its implicit aggression towards women and the almost tangible violence of the cultural, mental, social and (often) physical assault it visits upon them. In particular, it tells the story of a woman's encounter with pornography and the aggressive and predatory nature of men towards women. It follows her on a journey of ever accumulating psychological torment and disintegration, culminating in a breakdown when she pushes a man whom she suspects of following her, under a train.

This play 'pulls no punches' in the execution and development of its theme, and uses hard and uncompromising images, language and theatrical devices to make its point. The author is very clear in her assertion that she is dealing with a universal crime perpetrated by men upon women. Therefore, it is almost inevitable that a male actor or director, working upon the script, will feel alienated by its subject matter, the instinctive response being a defensive one against the ferocity of the play's attack. Indeed, many women find this play to be overly strident and judgemental in its approach. In fact, if this were a lesser play it would be tempting to dismiss it as a crude message, crudely stated. But this is a very good play and, as such, is tempered by wit and sincerity. Beneath the uncompromising surface lies a genuine core of humility and an understanding of humankind and the rigours of life generally. The breadth of the author's ability saves this from being simply a vulgar 'message' play and raises it to a completely different level.

The male actor or director (and perhaps the female too) must respond to this, check their instinctive feeling of combat and find the truths of the work and value them according to their worth and pertinence. There is absolutely no need for them to deny their own initial (or perhaps lasting) response to the play for this is valid and, paradoxically, productive within the three-way process.

There is much in this play to research: facts and figures, historical events, political movements and so on. This research, harnessed to balanced and sincere analysis and coupled to a respect for and commitment to the playwright's purpose (despite, but not ignoring, one's own possible views), should lead the theatre practitioner towards a true and exciting liberation of this play from the text to the stage.

This is research and analysis in practice – that is, finding of the truth in the work but also (and more importantly) a personal meeting between the artistic soul of the playwright and that of the practitioner.

GEOGRAPHICAL

The geographical setting of a play is all-important and also a vital area of research. An understanding of how a particular landscape can affect the lives of the characters that people it and shape the themes that underpin it, is of inestimable benefit.

A basic and vivid example of this point can be found in the translated works of world playwrights of the nineteenth century. Chekhov is an obvious choice here but colleagues such as Ibsen and Strindberg also wrote plays that contained a strong and influential sense of place and location at a national level.

However, be careful that you view geography in drama not just in terms of the broad, worldly and exotic sense but also in terms of the immediate, local and parochial. The physical area in which a play has its life can be of more significant and detailed importance than one might expect. Geography, in terms of drama, may be a country, a city or a village, but it may also be a room. It is possible to examine two significantly contrasting plays that rely upon very different (but equally important)

45

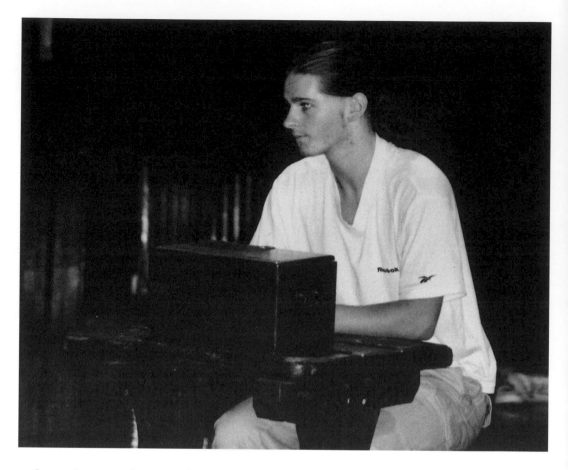

scales and types of geography in order to execute and empower their themes, along with another which mixes geographical setting, atmosphere and influence to great effect.

The action in Alan Ayckbourn's play *Woman In Mind* takes place in the open-air setting of a vicarage country garden. It is a summer's day, the sun is shining and the birds are singing: it is 'a geography' of seeming peace, freedom and relaxation. Such is the brilliance of drama (and perhaps art generally) that location is often used not to complement and enhance the theme, tone and intentions of the play but to juxtapose, conflict with and contrast with them, thus using the physical landscape to starkly illuminate the psychological landscape

A play inhabits a physical area.

with the deft use of subtle comparison: so it is with this particular work.

The characters that inhabit this garden – the vicar, his wife and sister – do not reflect the tranquillity, lightness or, indeed, openness of their surroundings, far from it. This is a play about narrow-mindedness, repression, lack of communication, unfulfilled lives and deep, festering resentments. Although a comedy, it is one of Ayckbourn's darker works, full of pain and anguish despite its hilarious approach. However, the themes of this play do not exist despite the setting but because of it. The shallowness and limitations of the characters' existence are highlighted by the place in which they find themselves and this affects them in different ways according to their particular mindset.

The vicar is complacent, unimaginative, narrow and lacking in true feeling. Therefore, for him, the garden represents contentment, safety and an ordered world in which he can live an unchallenged existence. His wife, on the other hand, is desperately frustrated and struggling with feelings of rejection and unworthiness. She sees the garden as a constant and ironic reminder of the contrast between the smooth, happy and uncomplicated life that she is supposed to enjoy – hosting 'jolly' vicarage tea parties on the lawn (passing around the cucumber sandwiches), for instance – and the bitter, stultifying bleakness of her personal existence in reality. Her environment, although just the same as his in a physical sense, is very different in terms of her relationship to it: it mocks her, taunts her with its banality and rubs salt into the wound of her very damaged and disturbed inner self.

It is to the differing influence of geography upon each character in this particular play (but generally applicable when considering all drama) that you should pay particular note. No one area of research and analysis exists in a vacuum and you must remember that probably the most effective way to research (and definitely to analyse) is to do so very much from the point of view of each character. If you are an actor then this will generally be angled towards the specific role you are playing, but directors must broaden their work and remember to filter their findings in differing (but cumulative) ways according to each individual that inhabits the geography of the play. Keep in mind that your work in terms of research and analysis (while somewhat academic in nature) is, in fact, wholly practical in essence, for its total and inclusive intention is designed to bring the words (that are its basic source mate-rial) to life; to give fictitious landscapes three dimensions and imaginary characters real bodies and minds to inhabit them. In this sense it is like no other study and is immensely rich and rewarding because of this.

A work in which geography, in the broadest sense, plays a very different role, both in its shape and influence, is *Rat In The Skull* by Ron Hutchinson. For much of the play there are three characters on stage, each of them very vividly drawn in terms of personality: a terrorist suspect, a senior policeman and a young constable. The play is set in the cell of a high-security police station and, as such, the setting is dark, small, claustrophobic and oppressive; the furnishings are suitably sparse, functional and basic – a table and two chairs. This is a work that takes an uncompromising look at the Northern Ireland conflict and the complexity of relationships and allegiances within it. The austere setting parallels the desperate situation of its characters, and the intensity of its geography mirrors the nature of their fractious and bitter encounter. Here can be observed theme, characterization and setting, all working in perfect harmony, each complementing and feeding off the other to produce an electrifying, stimulating and incredibly memorable atmosphere.

Apart from the very obvious illustration of the significance and influence of geographical setting, there is a very important point to be drawn from this example. There is clearly a need for research here: the very lifeblood of the play being anchored in its police cell environment requires it to be investigated in terms of realistic re-creation. However, there can be identified two distinct approaches to research in this context that (as ever) may be applied across a whole range of drama. One is a specific, detailed and accurate research into a room of this nature: its size, shape, location of windows, type of furniture used and the way in which it is set up. The other is a more generalized (but equally valid) approach into researching the feel, atmosphere and overall effect that such a room imparts and how this kind of environment shapes the events it hosts. To sometimes view research with this more symbolic outlook is not to escape the responsibility of accuracy in your work but to recognize the kind of accuracy that is required of you.

For instance, there can be no doubt that, were you to be working upon this play, visiting a police station to view the surroundings at first hand would be extremely valuable. However, it is important to appreciate this value for what it is and what it is not. Establishing physical accuracy from your visit may well be important but not essential (as this can be achieved equally well from reference material with less effort), but actually experiencing the sight, sound and smell of such a place is invaluable and totally unobtainable in any other way. After all, this is a location which, while familiar and appropriate to the characters involved, is not one in which you will usually (if at all) find yourself – a reaction to it cannot be experienced generally but only specifically. Thus searching out this specific experience through research is not only a requirement but uniquely enriching to you as a theatre practitioner.

Highlighted here too is the distinction between research into the factual and emotional influences of geography upon characters and the actors playing them. An understanding of the effects of environment upon the characters in *Rat In The Skull* can be effectively enhanced by literally researching the physical effects of the space upon the players. This can be achieved by rehearsing the scene in a more confined space than is normal or generally necessary, or restricting movement, albeit temporarily. Thus the sense of oppression and darkness can be created as a 'living' research that can be equally, if not more, valid than that of a more factual nature. This is one of the areas where improvisation meets research in order to promote analysis, and this

very practical approach to the subject will be discussed further in another chapter.

There is great and significant variety and contrast of geographical setting in Shakespeare's *King Lear*. While interior scenes may represent repression and restriction, they can equally represent security and safety. In *Lear* there is juxtaposition between the ordered and familiar world inside and the chaotic and uncontrollable landscape of the storm scene outside, mirroring Lear's personal journey in the play.

Many plays employ not only this type of significant variety of location but also a strong and poetic sense of 'place' in general. Many of Shakespeare's plays in particular evoke a powerful appreciation of setting related to theme, the geography becoming very much part of the overall impact created. Be it a forest, a castle, a wood, a sea, an island or a barren heath, each not only lays a solid foundation for the action to be played out but is also magnificently laden with the 'feel' of the drama and its themes and intentions. Every element contained in a good work of art (drama being no exception) should contribute to the overall effect, and setting is no exception.

It is difficult to imagine the play *Macbeth* without the massive contribution made to it by setting and the deeply affecting spirit of location it engenders: the dark, brooding castle echoing and reverberating with the very essence of murder, fear and evil. However, the theatre practitioner's appreciation of this play is not restricted, or hindered, by a specific adherence to particular bricks and mortar. Many interpretations of this (and other plays) may well place the action of the play in a different setting, both in the sense of place and, perhaps, time as well. Thus the castle may be translated into a military barracks, an underground nuclear shelter, a violent council estate or a post-apocalyptic wilderness. The important factor here is that the location reflects, parallels, identifies and empathizes with the original; it retains the same vivid, dramatic and vibrant truth relating to the atmosphere of place. This wonderfully highlights the importance of the essence of geography as opposed to the exact nature of it and must be remembered in all approaches to its research and analysis.

A very important part of your work is not only to understand the geographical elements of a play and to investigate them factually but

The importance of 'place'.

also to appreciate their significance and to become fully 'in tune' with the play's poetic sense of location. Geography in drama can create the right mood in an unsurpassable and inspirational way but, as with everything concerning drama, it is mood on paper, art in theory. It is nothing without the practitioner who brings it to the stage for the benefit of the audience. Therefore, if you are not in sympathy with its resonances it will fail.

In terms of character, geography may feature strongly in your research even when it is not immediately applicable to the actual play. It may be necessary to understand the area from which a persona comes and is brought up, even though the action may not be set there. Again, you should be looking to analyse the legacy of place upon the psyche of your subject as well as the physical consequences of factual detail. For instance, it will surely be just as useful and pertinent to your work to form an understanding of the psychological effects of a life spent as a miner, as it will to learn of the relevant causes and effects of lung disease. However, when your research and analysis will really begin to

take off and to pay dividends is when you can connect the two in a complete understanding of the part as a whole. The process of research for a theatrical practitioner will be about fact, but its purpose must always be about 'feel' – fact alone will never bring true understanding, and this is where your own personality and soul will enable you to be an analysing 'being' rather than a researching 'machine'.

CLASS AND SOCIAL STATUS

Society today is supposed, in theory, to be classless. In practice, the theatre practitioner knows that this is probably not true and, even if it were, he or she is often dealing with plays set in the past when it certainly wasn't.

Class and social status is an area of research and analysis that will undoubtedly cross-reference with others more than any. It certainly cannot be disassociated in any way from historical and geographical contexts. However, it is worth examining its importance individually, as it is vital to understand it both factually and emotionally when studying a play.

It is very likely that a play may focus much of its attention upon matters connected to this subject. To return once again to Shakespeare, *A Midsummer Night's Dream* is preoccupied with it in a very interesting way. One of the main reasons Shakespeare has not only stood the test of time as a great playwright but has also earned himself the title of 'genius' in the world of drama, is his ability to speak to modern dwellers of this earth, through the years, about issues that are not only frighteningly pertinent to them but which they can identify with on a very personal and instinctive level. In the *Dream* this is never truer than in the different levels and sections of society and beings that he illuminates. What gives this added zest is the fact that the highest of these strata – the upper class as it were – is comprised of the fairies, supernatural beings who believe themselves superior to all levels of mankind (this being especially true of Puck, the mischievous sprite). Below them are the ruling class of the humans (the posh people) and at the 'Bottom' of the pile (hilariously so) are the Rude Mechanicals – the working class – portrayed with great wit. The play clearly delineates the various 'classes' in terms of attitude, behaviour, response, communication, aspiration and endeavour. However (and this is where another part of the genius comes into play), it also emphasizes a strand of common ground that links humankind and, in this case, super humankind as well. All of the characters have energy, dynamism (of their own type) and a propensity towards the truly poetic – albeit to be found in different forms and at different levels of manifestation.

It is also well worth noting how Shakespeare is totally committed to all of the themes in his play and immerses himself in their realization and delivery. He does not only beautifully formulate the structure between these different types of existence by the use of language, dialogue, plot and situation but even manages to reflect it in a differing use of writing form: prose for the down-to-earth working men and verse for the more sensitive, sophisticated and educated characteristics of the upper echelons.

This play in particular, used as an example, brings home some very salient points about research of class and social standing and the analysis of it.

- Factual gathering of information about a particular class at a particular time and place must not only illuminate an understanding of the differences between the characters in a play (and perhaps the differences between a character you may be playing and the rest of their peer group) but also allow an equal understanding of what unites the people of a play; what thread pulls them towards an empathy with their mutual situation, whatever the drama has sanctioned this to be.
- Drama often achieves its aims without total (or even partial) commitment to detailed accuracy, reality or actuality of fact. It finds insight into its people, their situations and their lives, through a discovery of the underlying poetic and dramatic truth, rather than by rigidly applying a logical response to recognizable certainties. You must not only take this on board but should mimic it in your attitude and application towards your research and analysis of drama generally.

It may be fitting to close this chapter by pointing out that these points are as relevant to all areas of research as they are to the particular of class and social standing. By now you should be realizing that your work upon a play text is one of interesting and stimulating fact-gathering and, as a wonderful bonus, one of immense assimilation of understanding, appreciation, personal evaluation and dramatic revelation. An epicurean feast indeed!

4 HOW TO RESEARCH

PRECIOUS TIME

It is very rare indeed that you ever hear an actor, director, designer, stage manager, technician or anyone involved in the process of theatre say that they have too much time – or even enough time. It seems that a theatre production, almost by its very nature, will always be, if not rushed, certainly tightly scheduled. Although, as has already been established, most of your research as such will be conducted away from the main rehearsal process, and thus may be seen as additional work and time, there will still always be limitations upon the amount of effort you are able to expand on any particular production. The strains upon a theatre practitioner are great; directors will be involved in a good deal of administration work in addition to their artistic endeavours and actors will have the arduous job of learning lines (sometimes, by necessity, before rehearsals begin as well as during the rehearsal period).

Therefore it is vitally important that your research work is conducted in an as efficient and effective way as possible. There is no luxury of a long period of study here: the production process will demand strong, useful research, quickly delivered in manageable chunks, so as to facilitate rather than hinder the ongoing and demanding activity of raising a play and its character from the pages of a text and placing it in front of an expectant audience.

There are several primary sources and methods of research and it will be immensely useful to examine these in a way that will allow you to get the best out of them when needed in a practical situation. Thinking about, and experimenting with, the way in which effective research may be achieved in theory, away from the rigours of a real rehearsal situation, will help to greatly facilitate the process in practice, when often under considerable pressure.

It was established in the last chapter how important it is to understand the various areas of research, identify their real importance and apply oneself to them in the right way. Now it is time to see how this can be best achieved.

TRAVEL

When the actual location in which a play is set is important, in a world or national sense, then it is obviously advantageous to be able to visit this place to experience its geography and atmosphere at first hand.

At first thought, this may seem a luxury, indeed an indulgence that is beyond the scope of most theatre practitioners in terms of both time and affordability. Certainly, a play that takes place in a town a couple of hundred miles down the motorway would seem vastly more achievable and practical than an exotic location on the other side of the world; but, even if so, the effort involved can easily be seen as unnecessary and indulgent. It is a mistake to think this way, especially in the case of shorter, more accessible distances, but even when presented with the possibility of travel considerably further afield. Of course, it may well really be unnecessary and indulgent; the importance of researching a location in person must be assessed and quantified. There is absolutely no point in visiting a location,

however near or far, if the pertinence of the play's setting does not warrant it or the benefits outweigh the drawbacks.

For instance, a thriller set in a real and recognizable village somewhere in the countryside will probably not be particularly artistically dependent upon the actuality of the place but rather upon the general 'setting' of the village and its implications of a small and

Travel broadens an actor's mind.

concentrated community. In this case visiting it will probably be a waste of time, unless a director may wish to check geographical topography connected to the plot. Rather than research, the resources you require here are facilitated by your experience, education and emotional memory. As discussed before, the importance here is the practical and emotional 'feel' of a village (perhaps, in this case, in terms of its isolation), not any particular geography. Thus your research may be more 'improvisational' related to experience you may have of village life. (Having said this, if you have never spent time living in the countryside, a sojourn there may be helpful – but perhaps only when the quality of the play warrants it.)

However, a serious drama set, say, in India is much more likely to be directly and importantly dependent upon that country's landscape for its theme and purpose. This, again, will require evaluation, but there are many plays where the place in which the plot and action develop is of intrinsic relevance to the play as a whole. Be careful, though, not to equate importance with distance – a town not far from where you reside will be equally worthy of your research and first-hand exploration, if the quality, tone and relevance of the play indicates it to be so.

In terms of the shorter distances, laziness and prevarication will be your only enemies, and these must be beaten. If a place is research-worthy you need to spend some time, perhaps a day, finding out about it and seeing it for yourself. Once there make sure that you visit all the sights mentioned in the play and gather some useful information (or verify that which you already have). Drink in the sights and sounds; research is most definitely not just about facts and figures, so take time to absorb the experience of being in the place associated with the production on which you are working. Take tours and read guidebooks; look and listen; try to be sensitive to the atmosphere of each place that you visit; let the place find its way to your understanding of its significance to the play rather that to have a preconceived idea of its relevance.

The enemies of travel to farther and, perhaps, more exotic parts of the world, are easier to justify and harder to defeat. However, any reluctance you may have to undertake such journeys, and involve yourself in such research, may well just be a matter of perspective and attitude. The fact that you are reading this book means that you are serious about drama, to whatever degree you practise the art, and a serious theatre practitioner should consider structuring his or her life in a way that will help to develop their abilities. Therefore, it should not be beyond the bounds of reasonable dedication and application to choose and plan your holidays around your dramatic ventures. It is certainly easier on the psyche to consider that you have been prompted in your choice of vocational destination by the subject of a play that you are soon to be working on rather than thinking that you are making a special and expensive trip especially to research a play.

Holidays, notoriously stressful anyway, will take on a new sense of purpose and satisfaction when coupled to your work upon or behind the stage.

When planning and arranging these trips be sure to apply the same sense of budgetary caution that will inevitably be associated with most theatre productions. Look for good deals and choose sensible and not extravagant accommodation.

Wherever you travel, be it near or far, remember always that you are an artist working in an artistic field. As such, the atmosphere of place should always seem of more (although certainly not exclusive) importance to you than geographical or historical information.

THE LIBRARY

Drama people may be excused the no doubt biased opinion that a theatre is a temple of art, learning and human experience. However, even they grudgingly yield second place in importance to the great depositories of knowledge and understanding that are libraries. It is ironic, to say the least, that probably the most accessible institution to all of the population is often one of the most underused, and it may well be that theatre practitioners are often guilty of not making the most of such a wonderfully useful facility. Certainly, considering the frequency of library locations and the fact that they are a practically free resource (or, at least, with few additional charges beyond those financed from local taxation that has to be paid anyway), it is a wonder indeed that they are not crammed full of actors and directors all busy poring over masses of reference materials and queuing at the counter with armfuls of books to take out.

It may seem ridiculously obvious to instruct you to use your library more, both in general and for specific research projects, but it is surprising how many people in modern times do not instinctively see their local library as the first port of call when requiring information or when in need of solving an educationally based problem. Many teachers of drama are amazed at how students are not immediately or automatically tuned to the use of this resource and will even need prompting to utilize a library to just simply obtain a copy of a play that they are required to read. They do not seem to realize that, even though a book or script may be rare, it is possible to order it very easily and thus to obtain it relatively quickly. They are not aware that a library will not only contain databases of available material but talking, thinking human beings who are trained (indeed dedicated) to help in identifying useful and pertinent books and assessing their attainability. So visit your library as much as possible and allow your use of it to become a habit.

The library is thus an all-important facility in helping your research. Even the smallest of branches may contain a bewildering array of books and, unless you are researching a particularly unusual subject, many of these may contain information that will be of use to you. Therefore, the selection and filtering of your material must be a priority. Unplanned and unco-ordinated research is of no use and this is particularly so when facing a large and diverse selection of books that may be aligned to your area of interest but may also be of unquantifiable value and relevance initially. So think carefully about your choice of source material.

Considering that, for any given project, time will almost certainly be a dominating factor, it will be wise not to overload yourself either in terms of work or information. When presented with a selection of possible choices of books to read on any given subject it could be argued that to read several, many or even all of them would be advantageous in obtaining depth of knowledge and a balanced view of its relevance. While there is some truth in this, it is worth remembering that you are not an academic and you are not compiling a thesis. Your requirement is to obtain a sufficient (but not confusing) amount of material, suitable enough to enlighten and inform your practical work (which, after all is your primary objective in the first place), facilitate your analysis of character and situation, but without causing you to become bogged down in unnecessary detail and indulgent theory.

Assuming then, for the sake of argument, that time and effort restrictions require you to select just one book within a subject area to take away and read fully, you should consider carefully the following points in making your selection.

- Make sure that the book has either been written recently or been updated. There are few areas of knowledge that are not subject to change, addition and development and it is important that you are not misled by dated information. An old, respected and worthy tome may be invaluable to the scholar with more time for wider and more balanced study, but for your purposes current and fresh thinking will serve far better.

- Select a book that gives a balanced and unbiased assessment of the subject and not one that approaches it from a specific 'angle' or that attempts to prove or disprove a particular theory or argument. Your allegiance to the playwright's message and motives should lead you to enhance these with your own interpretation, analysis and portrayal. Of course the ideal is not to ignore other points of view but, when short of time, you must avoid clouding the issue with too much argument at the researching stage. The book should be talking to you directly, relevantly and without too much personal philosophy. On the other hand, the book should also have 'spirit' and verve and not just be a collection of arid and theoretical facts.

- Ensure that the author of the book is well qualified and experienced in terms of their topic. Read the short biography that is usually included on the flyleaf and try, as much as possible, to ascertain if the work is likely to be accurate and authoritative. Do not assume that the writer is a good enough expert without expecting them to justify the validity of their authorship with an appropriate background in the subject concerned.

- Look through the pages of the book and get a feel for its readability. The style of the prose should be simple, direct and informative. It should also communicate energy and enthusiasm for the subject and make you want to read on. The layout of the text upon the page should be accessible and inviting with clear and easily read print. As enjoyable as it may be, research is work and, like most work, the easier it can be made the better. Wading through dry and difficult-to-read pages will depress and discourage you. Try to find a book that will inspire and motivate you. Remember this point, too, when you are reading play texts, particularly classics: there is nothing worse than ploughing through a play (which is not essentially written to be read anyway) when the print is small and densely packed.

- Pick a book that contains useful and informative illustrations or photographs. This can shortcut the process considerably and enable you to absorb information more easily. However, be sure that these have been used selectively and that the book is not swamped with attractive but unhelpful distractions.

- If possible, find a book that has been recommended to you by a trusted colleague or friend. There really is no better way of avoiding a waste of time and effort than accepting advice. It is well worth asking around in order to find the right book and you will be surprised how often a useful suggestion will be forthcoming. However, make sure that your advisor understands what you are trying to research and why, and that they are in tune with your particular needs.

Of course, none of these points are hard-and-fast rules, and should be used selectively. However, a cumulative consideration of them should lead you to make the right choice. Do not forget to use the expertise of the librarians, ask their advice and do not be afraid to seek assistance if you are unable to work the database computers or have difficulty in accessing the information that you need.

If there is a particular book that you require, and it does not seem to be available, enquire about it and see if it can be tracked down and obtained for you. If you engage the staff in conversation about your needs and are a little pushy (in a polite and respectful way of course) you will often make discoveries and unearth gems of knowledge that might otherwise have been missed. If you are unlucky and encounter the gormless trainee or awkward 'jobsworth', ask to speak to the senior librarian or someone responsible for the library section applicable to your search.

If your research requires you to cross-reference material from several sources rather than from just one book you will probably want to visit the reference section of the library to conduct this work *in situ*. This is no bad thing as the studious atmosphere that a good library should possess will provide a focused and relaxed environment for your endeavours.

If this is the case, it is important that you go prepared. Have any additional research material with you and remember to take your notebook and pen or whatever apparatus constitutes your recording process. Try to pick a time when you will not be rushed or your mind occupied with other concerns. Be comfortably dressed and adequately fed and watered to sustain your concentration for a reasonable period prior to a break, which you should take at appropriate times so that you do not become fatigued and stale. Taking an occasional few minutes away from your studies will avoid your mind wandering when working, which is a waste of your precious time. Remain fresh and sharp, and when you feel yourself beginning to flag realize that it is time to stop and pack up. Like most activities, research is more effective when conducted in manageable chunks as often as possible, rather than long and tiring sessions of slog. Your most effective work will be done when you are firm but fair on yourself in terms of reasonable lengths of concentrated, disciplined study. However, don't let your breaks go on too long or you will find it difficult to get started again; get back to work, get on and get home!

When working to a deadline (as you may do) it will be tempting to work feverishly for long periods of time. Unless this is absolutely necessary avoid doing so, as it is likely that much of your effort will be wasted as your mind tires and fails to take in information and process it effectively. Remember that all of your work upon a play script should be fun, enlightening and enriching; try not to make it an ordeal for yourself.

As a final word about your work in libraries, be responsible for your part in retaining a studious and peaceful atmosphere for you and your fellow users. Turn off your mobile phone and, if working with a friend, only converse when necessary and at a low and considerate volume. Thus you will be helping to maintain this precious resource.

THE INTERNET

The Internet has revolutionized all our lives (or, at least, very few lives are now not touched by it in some way). The advances it has made in availability and (perhaps more importantly) accessibility are staggering and place it amongst the greatest of all inventions and innovations. In addition, along with other technological achievements, it has transformed communication and the transferring and sharing of ideas and information, both in terms of speed and ease of use. There are very few areas of life where it cannot be of service in some way or other, and the research of drama is certainly no exception.

If there were excuses that could be made in the past about the ability to find out and investigate any particular information, then there certainly is not now. Areas of research and study that used to be impossible, difficult or, at best, pretty inaccessible are now easily within reach, and questions that once seemed unanswerable, at least by anyone but an expert in the field, now give up their secrets at the touch of a keyboard or mouse. The Internet has empowered the user and facilitated the acquisition of knowlege for all those who are lucky enough to have access to it, and theatre practitioners are blessed by the opportunity to use it in their endeavours.

If you are a 'Luddite', and have no computer, you should seriously consider getting one. The constant fall in prices and increase of speed make them a considerable (and only occasionally frustrating and bewildering) tool. As an alternative, visit Internet cafés and facilities in the same way and with the same attitude as you

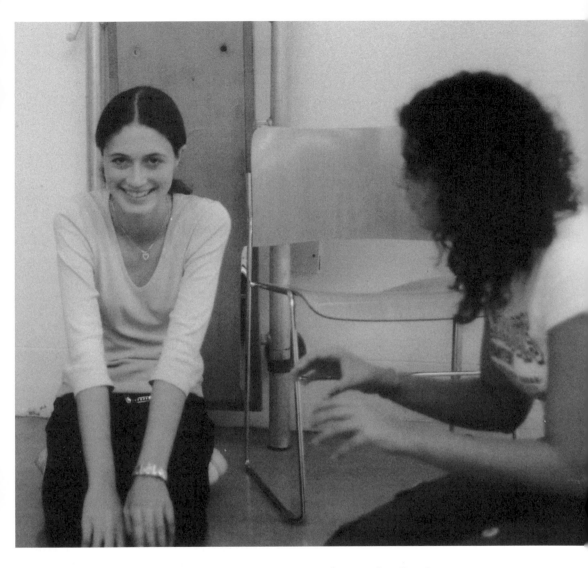

would have for libraries. For a little money you will have access to a universe of information while savouring a cup of coffee.

However, there is a problem – and that is the bewildering and potentially chaotic range and sheer volume of information available. If careful selection of source is important in a library, it is absolutely vital when 'on-line' in order to avoid being completely and incapacitatingly swamped.

Remember to take a break.

It is no accident then that the skill required in using the web is one of selection and discernment. Fortunately, there are devices built into the system with the sole purpose of enabling one to do this but these, in themselves, must be used carefully and thoughtfully in order to produce the best results.

The major tool available to you in this context is the 'Search Engine'. This will allow you to type in a word or phrase and list the various 'Internet Sites' that contain them, along with some idea of their general content. There can be literally thousands of suggestions and thus comes the danger of having too much choice to be productive within a limited time frame; also there are many of these searching facilities that are easily available and accessible (and their number grows all of the time). Two criteria emerge when considering them: which one to use and how best to use it in a way that will liberate your research rather than inhibit it.

At the time of writing most Internet providers have associated Search Engines easily

Research at the click of a mouse.

sourced from within their own software. In addition to this, others can be visited and utilized without problem by simply typing and entering an address. There are one or two known to produce particularly good results but, in the ever-moving world of cyber space, these may change, be added to or decline. Ask around amongst acquaintances who regularly 'surf the net' as to the best one to use. Failing this, a cursory glance through a few computer magazines will almost inevitably point you towards a reliable and productive search site.

Having done this, and with a screen in front of you with a box in which to enter your 'search' word or words, you must now pay a little attention as to what to enter in order, not only to obtain the best results, but also the most manageable ones.

However, before you even start, you should consider something very important. Internet searching and research, while innovative, does involve a considerable amount of moving from screen to screen and site to site. Therefore, it's beneficial to work with the fastest

---

Some Tips for Effective Searching

The following pointers will help you to produce the quickest and most useful information from your use of an Internet search facility.

- When searching using a particular phrase, such as 'to be, or not to be', make sure that you use quotation marks. This will cut down on extraneous and irrelevant results.
- Use the 'advanced search' facility wherever possible, as this will allow you to specify how current you wish the information be, and to also eliminate certain areas of information that the words you are entering might otherwise produce.
- You can use the plus and minus symbols on your keyboard to enlarge or limit the search respectively. For instance by adding + Shakespeare to 'to be or not to be' you will achieve results that only also mention Shakespeare (– Shakespeare would have the opposite result).
- To broaden a search effectively use the ~ symbol. This will then search for websites that contain synonyms of the word entered as well as the word itself. In other words, it will produce different words that mean the same thing.

---

form of Internet connection you can afford. Although faster speed may seem unnecessary when idly browsing through your favourite leisure sites, or even accessing your bank account, it will soon reveal its advantage when following trails of information across the web. The cumulative effect of sharper response times will make the whole process not only faster but more relaxing too, so invest in as fast a system as you can.

The key to successful 'searching' is twofold. Firstly, to be very precise in deciding exactly what you want to know and the results that you expect and, secondly, to enter words that contain both the general and the precise in terms of what you require while also eliminating the extraneous, thus producing results that will provide useful choices without leading you off into irrelevance.

THE INTERVIEW

It has already been established that drama is a unique art form by the fact that it uses life itself – real actors giving life to real human embodiments of expression – in order to deliver its artistic and poetic communication. It is no coincidence then that probably the most effective, productive and constructive research that can be undertaken when working upon a script is that of personal connection with people willing and able to contribute to an understanding of the play. If you are able to identify anyone who has knowledge about your subject matter (either directly or indirectly) and they are prepared to give you a little of their time, then you should grasp the opportunity with relish. A living, breathing, talking human being is more likely to give a unique and invaluable insight into the project than any amount of written words (or any other kind of research) is ever likely to do.

The word 'interview' in this context suffices as a means of identifying the type of research, but it will not always be appropriate as a method of approaching it. It may well be that, in some instances, a formal (albeit friendly) interview is the best way of extracting the information you require but, more often then not, an informal 'chat' and relaxed conversation will produce better results, and this is certainly the best way of looking at the process. Very often an opportune exchange with an appropriate person you already know can provide more usable research than an arranged meeting with someone you do not.

Personal contributors to your research will fall into two main groups: those who have a knowledge of the subject matter of your play (to whatever degree) and (in cases of real-life themes) those who have direct experience of the actual story. In the latter case, the individual you are talking to might even be the person you are playing or the central character in a dramatization you are directing and, if so, the particular usefulness of this is priceless. Such persons, along with all those who have a first-hand appreciation of the subject matter, will provide strong and reliable factual source material, but there are others who will also be able to impart a great deal of background research in their capacity as experts in the area generally and these are very often just as valuable for your purposes.

However, it will be helpful to examine first your approach to a person who was a part of the real story or may even be the person about whom the play was written. The reason for dealing with this type of interviewee before others is that while providing obviously rich uniquely revealing insights into the reality of the play, they also pose a possible risk to your endeavours.

This is mainly because they represent a strong addition to the 'three-way process' that was elucidated in Chapter 1. True, this can be an immensely valuable addition, but it could also be one that perverts and derails the process. While the risk is worth taking it is also worth understanding it in order to avoid the implications of it. The best way to do this is by first remembering a parallel example from another art form.

When a painter visits a particular landscape in order to paint it, they should do so, not with the intention of simply re-creating the scene in factual and recognizable detail, but in terms of capturing what they, as thinking and feeling individuals, actual see in the scene and what it means and says to them. This is then passed on, within the process, to the observer of the picture who draws upon this and allows the work to stimulate their own unique response, maybe in accord with or maybe quite different (in part or total) from that of the artist. The observer may decide that, as they enjoy the painting so much, they wish to visit the site and observe the same scene for real. In doing this they may add to their understanding, enjoyment and appreciation of the painting. However, they may spoil it, finding that the actuality of the landscape detracts or even destroys their personal reaction to it on the canvas. Certainly, their relationship with the picture and its artist is very likely to be changed – either for better, worse or perhaps a mixture of the two.

Within the three- rather than two-way process of drama, this same principle can become a real danger when it can affect the actor or director in the additional middle part of the process. For your purposes the play script represents the painting. Your reactions to it, as it reveals itself (perhaps uniquely) to you from the page, are vital. It is your development of these reactions that enables you to bring the character or characters to life. Although the story you are dealing with may be real, you are still associating with it within an artistic process and it is your human interpretation of the text that allows this process to work. The playwright has given you the facts about a story and the characters that people it, but it is your illumination, humanization and realization of these facts that give the drama power to inform, stimulate and affect an audience. Additional information and insight, while being superbly enriching to the process, can also distort and disarm its artistic core if you are not careful.

So you must ensure that, when meeting and speaking to people closely or directly associated with the story of the play, you remain objective and selective about the information that is useful to you and that which, regardless of its obvious truth, is not. Keep in mind that certain information may give you an additional insight into the play that might not only be irrelevant but also distract or prevent you from communicating the true voice and intention of the piece.

Real people make the best research subjects.

Your first and foremost responsibility is to the playwright and their work. Your intention must be to allow your humanity to communicate their ideas and thoughts, albeit filtered and embellished through your own involvement with them, in as faithful and true a way as is possible. Therefore, do not forget that a real person, intimately involved in the story, may not see it in the same way, may not be in accord with the author's perspective upon it, may not draw the same conclusions from it or may even disagree with its factual details. Indeed, they might be opposed to the particular interpretation that the play places upon the story or even its telling in the first place. If this is the case then while it may be unfair to expect the information they impart to be untrue, it would not be unreasonable to presume it to be tainted or, at least, subjective in its substance.

There is no real problem here, and you should certainly not be discouraged from searching out and utilizing such worthy research material, but you must keep these factors in mind and view everything you learn with an impartial eye and the play and the playwright always as your main point of reference and source of authority. As with all research, interviewing must complement the process, not dominate it.

When researching in this way, whatever the degree of knowledge or personal involvement with your subject matter that the contributor may possess, there are some simple, but vitally important, details to consider when talking to them. By thinking about the best way to approach your discussion beforehand rather than just 'diving in' regardless, you will not only get the best out of them but also avoid missing the most vital pieces of information they can impart. So reflect upon the following points.

- Make sure that this is a discussion and not just a long list of questions to be fired at your subject, expectant of quick and precise answers. Very often the information you require will not necessarily be in the forefront of your contributor's mind – they may not even realize they possess it at all. Therefore a gentle two-way exchange will slowly but surely extract better results.

- Connected to the point above, do not have too many notes: a list of questions constantly referred to upon a page will be off-putting. Use your theatrical skills to remember the important points you want to cover and use notes sparingly.

- Make sure that your contributor is relaxed. Try to arrange a time to meet them when they will not feel rushed. Make sure they are comfortable and have something to drink (and eat if appropriate), and pick an informal and quiet venue for the meeting.

- Be mindful of the amount of personal involvement a contributor may have with the subject and particularly careful if their recollections might involve them emotionally. You will not reap many rewards in terms of useful research if they are unduly upset or angered. On the other hand, it will be acceptable (and perhaps fruitful) to gently allow them to become emotionally engaged with their answers, provided this is done carefully and (above all) sensitively. Do not avoid difficult subjects (for they are the ones you are most likely to be interested in) but treat your contributor with respect and understanding. Asking 'what was it like to see your friends killed in battle?' is not likely to get you very far, but a delicately guided conversation will probably eventually reveal that very information, and it is this level of personal and human insight (as opposed to simple facts) that is your very stock in trade.

- Try to strike a balance between keeping the exchange relaxed and non-confrontational, at the same time keeping your contributor on the point and focused. Make sure that you do not lose potential information by being too 'nice' and easygoing. It is important to dig into what they have to say and prompt and encourage them to divulge as much as possible. Provided you do this politely and approach the topics with integrity you should flatter them with your interest rather than offend them. However, never push too hard and try to know when to stop and change the subject. Remember that, however effusively someone may be talking, they will soon 'dry-up' if they feel under pressure. Do not spoil hard-won enthusiasm by carelessness.

- In the same way that referring to notes can be off-putting, so can making them. Obviously, this will need to be done in some way, but keep your focus on the person and try to make your recording of what they have to say as simple and unobtrusive as possible. Do not keep them waiting while you laboriously write everything down as this will interrupt their flow and inhibit them, which is exactly what you want to avoid. So use some kind of personally understandable shorthand and write up your notes properly at a later time.

- You will probably be pleased and grateful for the help that you are being given, but do not forget to show it. Leave the person in no doubt as to the validity of their contribution, and make sure that they feel appreciated and connected to the project. Ask them to see the play as your guest and tell them that you will be seeking their opinion of it afterwards. You never know when you might need their help again either for another project or to check or develop something they have told you, later in the rehearsal process, so part on good terms and with a positive feeling of success about the exchange. Not all of this type of research is fruitful and, if the meeting has not been as productive as you hoped or perhaps even a waste of time, do not allow this to show: you may need this person's help, in better circumstances, in the future.

Recording an Interview

By far the best way of recording (and completely negating the problems of note writing) is to tape a research-based conversation in its entirety and transcribe it at leisure. This will also allow you to replay the interview and confirm or revisit important facts and (more pertinently) inferences. It is surprising how instant interpretation and the unreliability of memory can lead to misunderstanding or dubious conclusions. Having the ability to relive the conversation immediately afterwards or at a later date (perhaps several times if you wish) will be invaluable and promote far greater accuracy of research. However, it is vitally important that you seek the contributor's permission to do this and use an unobtrusive recording device so as not to inhibit them. They may be a little self-conscious at first, but they will soon forget that they are being recorded provided they had no objections to it in the first place and that no formality is created by using too large or complex a machine. By the same token, make sure you know how to work it properly, as great amounts of 'fiddling' with it will not be helpful.

MUSEUMS, ART GALLERIES AND REFERENCE FACILITIES

In the same way that actually speaking to a person involved with your project is uniquely enlightening, so is the physical encounter with the multifarious artefacts and exhibits contained in the countless institutions that are dedicated to art, literature, history, science and all kinds of knowledge in their colourful diversity of form.

A visit to your local town or, if possible, your nearest city should provide you with a surprising number of locations and opportunities to

research. To see, hear or perhaps even touch articles related to your quest is wonderfully enriching and extremely enjoyable also. There is, of course, some effort involved, and maybe a little expense too, but it is well worth the investment of both.

This type of research will obviously be of most use when the play you are working on has an historical theme, or when it takes as its hero or heroine an important historical figure. Dramatic literature is often concerned with the stories of great artists and the complexities of

Living museums are the best.

their lives. To be able to browse through their work in the comfort of a gallery or exhibition will roll back time, help to connect you to them across the years and provide an illuminating window into their very psyches and souls. There is no finer research for the actor or director than that which, apart from giving them a factual understanding of the play, brings them towards a closer and more intimate empathy with the characters they are committed to bringing to life.

In the same way, to be able to examine the type of furniture, clothes and everyday objects associated with the period and location of the play is equally fascinating. To actually come face to face with part of the world inhabited by your subjects in a museum will supply you with a far greater appreciation of who they are and how to play them than any amount of factual reading. Most cities have a variety of museums that supply a wide scope of knowledge across many areas of research, and most towns (and indeed some villages) will contain smaller establishments specializing in more local history. Many museums are free to enter but, despite this, may be much under-used. A visit to a museum is highly enjoyable as well as educational, and your research objectives should be used as a marvellous excuse to spend some time in them.

However, it cannot be denied that often it is pure fact-finding that will drive your research. For example, details of births, deaths and marriages may well be needed to complete your picture of a real-life family or provide background material for the real life setting of an otherwise fictitious story. In this case, the public records offices and other research facilities, both local and national, will be of use to you. Conversely, if you need to investigate a particular event, the archives of newspapers could be appropriate hunting grounds.

Remember that many of these facilities may be available on the Internet and, being places of pure factual reference, will not necessarily reveal any more by being personally visited. However, it is worth remembering also that the physical sites of such institutions will be peopled whereas the 'virtual' ones will not. A real person to guide you to the best departments and areas (and perhaps even divulge some information themselves) can be invaluable and will at least shortcut the process for you.

Certainly, the web might prove a good starting place when identifying and locating potential sources, but if you do then decide to visit, it will be well worth telephoning first to establish up-to-date opening times and any special requirement for their use.

Do not overlook the less obvious places of potential research and fact-finding. Churches can often prove treasure troves of information with their plaques, records and inscriptions. There has also been a fair amount of fruitful research conducted in graveyards, where tombstones can reveal a wealth of interesting detail and often provide links in piecing together the history of a particular family, village or town. Cathedrals can be even more revealing in terms of broader and less parochial knowledge. Long-established local businesses and shops can divulge a wealth of background knowledge about a specific location, and taxi firms, train stations and bus companies can often provide precise and useful geographical information.

THEATRES AND CONCERT HALLS

It is easy to overlook this area of research as it is so closely aligned with your primary purpose in the first place. In the same way that theatrical works sometimes deal with the lives of great visual artists, so do they too in the case of musicians and even playwrights themselves. Therefore, attending concert halls and theatres to sample their work will be of great and enjoyable benefit.

Also, when working upon a play, while you may want to avoid attending a performance of another production of the same play (for obvious reasons), other plays by the same author may be interesting to see and can provide more insight into a canon of work than simply reading the scripts.

Immersing yourself in the performance arts (not forgetting dance also) is of extreme importance, not only in terms of research upon specific projects, but as an ongoing discipline for your artistic development generally. However, this can be expensive, especially in the more prestigious venues and amongst the worthier companies, but this does not necessarily need to discourage you, even if you are on a tight budget. Many theatres and other performance arenas will have concessionary rates for certain categories, so check to see if you fall into one of these. This may be particularly applicable if you are a student, unemployed or of more senior years. Additionally, they very often operate a policy of selling off unsold or returned tickets at discounted rates shortly before a performance (sometimes highly discounted). Although this may involve you in some queuing, and attending a venue in good time to do so effectively, it is well worth it and making a habit of this will reduce your expenses tremendously.

Telephone all the venues local to you to see if they provide any of these cost-cutting schemes. If they do not, try to persuade them to do so.

Holiday planning can come in to play here as well. Organizing a trip around a visit or visits to a performance or performances can lead to a wonderfully rewarding vacation.

READING

While this heading has obvious connections to the consideration of libraries earlier in this chapter, it is worth examining the benefits of reading as such, especially in terms of fictional rather than just reference work research.

If the hero or heroine of the play you are working on was (or is) a real writer then you will obviously want to read at least some of their work: it is difficult to portray greatness without experiencing that which created the greatness in the first place.

However, your main area of concern when considering your reading habits must be that of drama both in general terms and especially in regard to the other works of the playwright you are working on at any particular time. A good general rule here is to make the regular reading of drama a habit. 'Regular' is the keyword here – even if you only read one play that is new to you each week, you will soon build up an impressive knowledge of dramatic literature. With this kind of ever-growing background expertise you will discover that, with each production you embark upon, either as actor or director, you will be more and more preconditioned to the study of it by your previous knowledge of the playwright and their work. This does not mean to say that you can happily avoid a rereading of as many of the author's catalogue of plays as possible when working upon a particular one. However, it does mean that the process will be made easier by your established knowledge, and this will enable you to view the works much more in the context of particular ideas and themes that may be beginning to emerge in your treatment of the production rather than just simply finding out what they are about and understanding them each from scratch.

It is worth reconfirming that, time and time again, students of drama and, very often, established practitioners fail to fulfil their potential because they do not possess sufficient knowledge about the playwright in question. In addition, such a person is also prone to make a bad and slow start to a rehearsal process because they have not read the actual play upon which they are to work, enough times or with sufficient care.

However, it is important not to get this out of proportion. A theatre practitioner does not need to have an encyclopaedic knowledge of drama or be a professor of dramatic literature. Yours will always be a practical vocation but it is one that must be backed up by a good and reasonable workable knowledge of

text. The requirement is to be widely but modestly well read, thus to be equipped with a good means of starting work upon any play from a firm standpoint and without too much of an initial shockwave of effort.

This is not difficult to achieve and, if it is an area in which you know yourself to be weak,

Use holidays wisely.

start to do something about it now. Regular (but not excessive) reading will soon begin to reap rewards both in terms of your ability and confidence.

67

5 DIFFERENT TYPES OF DRAMA

DIFFERING NEEDS

One of the most exciting and absorbing features of drama is the vast wealth of material that there is to practise upon. However, not only is there a countless selection of plays on which to apply your skills of research, analysis and interpretation, but also a wide range of different types of work, each with its own very different style and challenges.

Each basic category of drama presents the theatre practitioner with different challenges, approaches to the work, requirements in terms of research and methods of analysis. Because of this it will be useful for you to have an overview of some of the important categories in terms of the demands they will place upon you and the tools you will need in order to do them justice.

In general, the different types and styles of dramatic works can be identified and divided by their place in history and the world. In other words, a category or style will normally appertain to a particular historical period, geographical region or (perhaps most often) a combination of both. There is, of course, some crossover and blurring of distinctions but, fundamentally, it will be possible for you to look at these groupings within broad distinctions and thus have a clear idea of the work and application of

OPPOSITE: *Mr Punch has an impressive pedigree.*

technique needed for each. Therefore, there follows a section on some major groups with an insight into the kind of approach and application that will be needed in their study.

GREEK THEATRE

This earliest example of formalized theatrical performance is full of epic tales, dramatic themes and large, colourful characters. It is usually gigantic in scale, highly charged emotionally and bold in its storytelling. There are many and varied roles and (supporting these actors, but also of vital importance) a dramatic 'chorus', narrating, illuminating and commenting upon the action.

The stories are based upon myths and legends, gods and deities. This early and formative theatre starts as it means to continue by concerning itself with momentous struggles between good and evil, life and death, man and god. It bombards its audience with all the recognizable emotions of joy, fear, pain, sorrow and hope that constitute human existence. Thus it begins a tradition that will persist through the ages of reflecting this existence back to mankind and helping, through an artistic process, to allow an understanding of its mysteries. However, though there may be subtlety and minutiae within its content, there is little in its presentation. Performed in large amphitheatres to vast crowds of onlookers, it is gigantic in scope, loud, fast and extremely powerful.

At the root of this power are the stories themselves and this must obviously be the foremost focus for research. While, as always, the script will inform you of the plot, you must investigate, through your various sources already identified, the significance of the story, its importance and the reasons for its telling. You will need to investigate its historical details and to ascertain how much of it is based in fact, how much in legend and how much in fiction. You will also need (and perhaps most importantly) to gain an understanding of the traditions and beliefs that spawned it. Remember that the original audience for this type of theatre were a people whose lives were governed, influenced and controlled by their belief in various gods and an adoration of and sublimation to their powers. Greek theatre is heavily rooted in this and you will need not only knowledge of the stories and legends but also an understanding of what they meant to the recipients of them.

It is at this point that analysis, alongside research, begins to play its part in earnest. Your responsibility in terms of audience is, of course, to the modern day one that will receive your interpretation of the work. Therefore, you must translate your understanding of the importance of the story to the ancient Greeks into a strategy for highlighting its relevance to an array of twenty-first-century onlookers.

The imposing scale of Greek theatre.

There is a great deal of truth in the adage that very little changes through time, and much of the content will remain totally appropriate; mankind today shares many of these thoughts, emotions and concerns. However, the way in which they manifest themselves and the context in which they are understood is different.

For example, modern men and women may now have more refined belief systems and ones that are based less on superstition and ignorance, but the balances between good and evil, light and dark, god and man are still basic fundamentals of all world religions, and, in an age when religion is less dominant, also important issues as such to atheists and agnostics alike.

Another example can be found in weather and environmental change. Storms, tempests, famine and flood may now be seen more in terms of issues of mankind's stewardship of the planet and less in terms of godly wrath and damnation upon the world, but the monumental importance of their effect upon life (and indeed death) remains very much the same and their influence is still greatly worthy of exploration in dramatic form. Such power echoes in all life.

Your work then must be to recognize and investigate the parallels that exist here, to

Oedipus – intense tragedy.

The Power of *Oedipus*

As an exercise in the examination of Greek Theatre, look at the story *Oedipus* as told by Sophocles and imagine how you would interpret its violent power for a modern-day audience. In doing so ask yourself the following questions:

1. In the story, Oedipus consults and is guided by the Oracle. In modern society what has replaced the Ancient Greek's reliance and faith upon external superstitious influences? Are there now new 'Oracles' and are they as all-pervading as those of former civilizations? If so, how can their relevance be best communicated to an audience?

2. What effect will the themes of sexual violence and incest have upon a modern audience? Do these subjects still command the same power and attention as they have through previous centuries? If so, how can this best be dramatized to ultimate effect? If not, how can an audience, sated with a modern predilection for scandal and intrigue, be made to feel a renewed horror for these elements of the drama?

understand the mutual significances that exist across the time divide since the plays were written and to find a way of interpreting them that will lead a modern audience towards an appreciation of them that is not only historically interesting but also relevant to their own lives. It is plain to see that this must be a question not of changing the work, for that would be to unforgivably disregard your relationship with the playwright (however long dead they may be), but of slanting, angling and proffering it in a way that will enable it to do its work of speaking freshly to yet another new generation. Remember that great works from this and every other period of dramatic literature have existed beyond their own time because of their universal relevance and appeal, but this has not happened without countless generations of theatre practitioners who have been equal to the task of interpreting them in new and imaginatively relevant ways. Do not underestimate your part in this process of preservation.

Medieval Theatre

Medieval theatre developed from Christian liturgy and was used all over Europe as a religious story-telling device and instructional tool, growing from simple acts of faith to large and colourful pageants.

In England the 'Mystery Plays' told the story of Jesus Christ and concerned themselves with moral elucidation and instruction. In understanding these texts today, the practitioner will need not only to research their religious significance at the time they were first performed, but also the implications of where they were performed.

The original settings for these plays were the churches. Of particular interest here is the way in which the whole church would be utilized as a performance space, with certain areas used for particular formulaic parts of the plot and theme. For instance, the area of the church to the left of the altar, as the congregation (or audience) would look at it (stage right), would always represent heaven and the area to the right from their angle (stage left) would represent hell. Thus God, Jesus, prophets and all manner of 'good' people would appear and speak their lines from stage right, while stage left was reserved for the devil and all his many minions.

A little analysis of this grouping can reveal fascinating relevancies with modern times both in terms of church and theatre. Stage right (as it were) in a church still remains the unfailing location for the pulpit from which the priests and preachers usually preside while stage left is the preserve of laymen and women as they read from the lectern situated there. Perhaps there can be seen a tenuous reason why some modern and more evangelical preachers prefer to stand in the middle of the church – an area that was used for the general and more neutral scenes in the Mystery Plays. In the same way, in pantomimes today, the Good Fairy will always enter from (and should remain) stage right, and the Wicked Villain (in whatever manifestation) from stage left – a direct reference point to early theatre.

Further general significance can be noted from the fact that the plays gradually moved out and away from the churches, to be played out and about. This was almost certainly partly because of the increasing size and scale of the productions and a loss of simplicity, but also due to the increased bawdiness of the content becoming less than appropriate for a pious setting. Here can be seen the first signs of drama expanding and developing both in terms of its ambition and production values and its progressive movement away from its religious beginnings towards encompassing a wider and more secular remit of human existence and experience.

So here can be found much scope for study, not just in terms of understanding and

performing the texts involved, but also from the point of view of appreciating what modern theatre has inherited from these theatrical times. Of course, any period or type of theatre will reveal foundations for future generations and movements of drama, but this can be quite clearly seen in this very early and seminal form of 'national' theatre.

However, there are other very interesting areas for your research, most of which are firmly based upon enabling a worthy, modern portrayal of this work.

- The plays were often written in 'cycles' related to certain areas of the country. An examination of their content and construction will lead to an appreciation of their importance.

Medieval drama – the origins of Open Air Theatre.

- Immediately after leaving the church environment the plays were presented directly outside, often with the church doors used as a backdrop to the scenes. However, this later expanded geographically and often the scenes would be staged upon carts, which would be assembled in loose formation in areas of a town before repeating the performance in a different location. Here can be seen and studied early forms of informal presentation of plays and the forerunners of such incarnations as 'theatre in the round' and 'promenade performance'. Certainly, this was theatre for the people by the people and therefore can reveal huge relevancies to modern concepts of theatre today.

- The plays often contained quite complex effects and scenery, along with elaborate costume, and had generally high production values. Thus, despite a very immediate and down-to-earth relationship with the audience, these players were committed to, and very serious about, the drama and its presentation. It is interesting to explore the energetic dynamics of production in bringing these colourful stories to life.

- There was a very strong comic-based characterization, with performances clearly drawn and broadly funny in order to appeal to and connect with the townsfolk of which the audience was comprised. This provides a strong and down-to-earth approach to the acting techniques required for this type of outdoor, informal and itinerant production.

COMMEDIA DELL'ARTE

Part of the Italian renaissance, this fascinatingly and highly comic type of theatre is hugely formulaic and fascinating to study and unravel.

Strictly speaking this is more a case of researching background and style rather than actual text as this was improvised rather than script-based work and therefore a practitioner today, working in this style, would either be improvising too or working with a play constructed around the essence of the form rather than a direct translation of text.

The unique factor here is that each performer would play a certain and particular character in each and all of the different stories that would be presented. These stock, individual and highly recognizable characters would remain constant, while the plot and theme in which they were placed would alter along very thematic lines. This, coupled to the impromptu nature of the

play construction, made for a form that was uniquely based and dependent upon the actor rather than playwright. In this sense there is an obvious loss of the 'three-way process', but this is made up for by the immensely inventive, stimulating and exciting improvisational way the stories were explored and brought to life.

There are great lessons to be learned by a director from *Commedia* in terms of collaborative devising and, for an actor, the exploration of one character within varying and ever-changing scenarios is an extremely useful discipline.

From a practical angle, practitioners confronting this type of work will need to research diligently the type and quality of movement that is required, This kind of theatre was, in many ways, a forerunner of what today is loosely termed 'Physical Theatre' and requires not only a loose, strong and responsive physicality but also a clear concept of communicative, energetic and, above all, economic expression of movement.

There is also great scope for cross-referencing here as *Commedia* has been influential in many types of theatre and entertainment generally. This ranges from huge elements of silent cinema – such as Charlie Chaplin and The Keystone Cops – to the still highly popular *Punch and Judy* shows, where the character of Mr Punch is a direct descendant of Punchinello (a prominent character from the *Commedia* repertoire).

RESTORATION THEATRE

In 1660, when Charles II returned to England, it heralded a new start in English theatre and a restoration of a dramatic culture that had been totally suppressed during the Civil War. Theatres had been closed, plays forbidden and actors outlawed and, after eighteen years of neglect, both the physical and intellectual infrastructure of theatre was in a parlous state.

The restoration of theatre saw new and magnificent buildings for the purpose of entertainment, and enthusiastic and newly liberated audiences, ready and eager to make theatre-going fashionable again. At first they had to be content with the rehashing of old plays, as companies returned and venues opened. However, before long new and exciting drama was being written. This consisted mainly of bawdy comedies of manners – known collectively as Restoration Comedy. Playwrights like Wycherley, Congreve, Vanbrugh and Farquhar (particularly known for the boisterousness of his plays) were soon thrilling audiences with their audacious plots and vividly drawn larger-than-life characters.

This was, of course, a very exciting time for theatre and there is much historical information that can be researched in terms of the plays, the theatres in which they were performed and the companies (and their directors) who produced them.

In terms of understanding the texts from this period from a performance point of view, the main emphasis is thrown upon the very particular style required in bringing 'page to stage'. This style is both physical and vocal and its acquisition is based upon an understanding of the content of the plays in terms of society manners and social interaction. Performances within Restoration Comedy are 'large' (both in terms of gesture and characterization generally), openly expressive and loquacious, and therefore the actor requires a strong, relaxed and flexible technique in terms of both their 'instruments': body and voice.

The best way of obtaining and facilitating the style, physicality and vocal agility required for this very demanding drama, is to learn and practise it directly through classes. This is a skill that, while it may be identified by reading and other theoretical research, cannot be utilized and perfected without experiencing it directly under tuition. If you have difficulty in finding a suitable class, it would be wise to seek out an expert in the form who would be willing to impart advice and guidance. Directors, too, should be fully cognizant with all aspects of the style and be able to help actors practically in the same. Whatever happens, make sure that you do not undertake a piece of this kind without adequate research and practice. These comedies stand or fall by the performers being able to apply the style expertly, precisely and with a lightness of touch.

Acting in a Restoration Comedy requires not only a generosity of performance but great precision and deftness too. Almost more importantly, it requires a cultural understanding of the traditions, affectations and social conventions of the time that motivate the style. Therefore, you should begin your quest to become practitioners of these texts by researching the various aspects thoroughly and relating them to the type of movement and vocal agility that will be needed. You will also find a kind of upper-class slang pervading the text, and the use of this and its significance in social intercourse must also be understood.

NINETEENTH- AND TWENTIETH-CENTURY DRAMA

This may seem a very wide and expansive grouping and in terms of academic study it most certainly is. However, from the point of view of your purposes in understanding text it is a useful one by the fact that through this arbitrary, vastly varied period there runs a common theme that is of significance to a study of text in terms of performance. This is a growing and developing use of ideas-based drama; that is, plays that increasingly deal with an examination of the human condition and interaction within society. The fashion for the thematic and issue-driven drama of today has had its gradual establishment over a long and evolving period, and throughout these two

The 'truth' of realism.

hundred years examples can be seen of playwrights pushing the boundaries of their day in terms of creating thought-provoking work based upon reflecting the concerns, problems and, in many cases, triumphs of their various ages.

This is a world-wide phenomenon, and can be seen in the works of Chekhov, Ibsen, Strindberg, Wilde, Shaw, Coward, Arthur Miller, Tennessee Williams, Brecht, Pinter, Wesker, Edward Bond, David Hare, Alan Ayckbourn, Michael

The Importance of Chekhov

While all of the major playwrights of the last two centuries are exemplars, it is worth paying particular attention to Anton Chekhov. He was substantially influential in promoting a more realistic and naturalistic approach to drama, and his connection with Stanislavsky of the Moscow Arts Theatre (the director of many of the original Chekhovian productions and the most famous acting teacher of all time) makes his work especially relevant to you.

Chekhov is the master when it comes to the mult-layering of text and the strong influence of subtext (the deeper meanings that lie beneath the obvious definition of the words).

Over a period of time you should endeavour to read or see his five major plays: *Three Sisters, Uncle Vanya, The Cherry Orchard, The Seagull* and *Ivanov*. Pick an appropriate character from one of these and, as an exercise in identifying and playing subtext, focus upon the motivations and real meanings behind everything that the characters say. Think also of the effect of the environment upon them and how the brewing atmosphere of change and faded gentility that the plays project affect their thinking.

Frayn and Tom Stoppard to name but a few. All of these playwrights represent a progressive movement towards a greater importance of the text itself and a growing emphasis upon naturalism in both setting and performance.

You should read some examples of the works of all those authors mentioned (and more). In doing so it will begin to become clear that drama based upon ideas and human experience cannot be researched and analysed purely externally of yourself.

Understanding leads to emotional release.

These kinds of play require the practitioner to look inwardly too, in order to discover what the content means to them, how it affects them and how they relate to it. As you do this you will be learning the most important lesson of all: that understanding text is also about understanding yourself. This is because you are the tool that must be essentially used when bringing a script alive; you are the raw material that transforms the writings of another into a living reality upon the stage. Any amount of study and analysis will be useless to you if you make the mistake of leaving yourself out of the equation.

6 RESEARCHING AND ANALYSING SHAKESPEARE

A SUBJECT IN ITSELF

Such is the quality and importance of Shakespeare's Theatre, an overview of it in terms of the subject matter of this book requires it to have a chapter dedicated to itself. This is not to suggest that what you will learn here will not be applicable to other types of drama – both those contemporary to Shakespeare and those of other periods and cultures – it most certainly will be. However, the sheer weight and quality of possible study is so significant as to make Shakespeare a subject apart, fully encompassing in itself, while reflecting its treasures most usefully on all others.

You will need time with this chapter in order to appreciate the skills and techniques needed to be a fully functioning interpreter of this great man's work. However, it is time well spent, as it will empower you to approach every part of your work with confidence and insight.

A PARTNERSHIP OF SKILLS

In order to fully explore the techniques involved in researching and analysing drama it becomes inevitable that the two disciplines are very often examined separately. Indeed, there are occasions when their application becomes, to a certain extent, separated too. However, on

OPPOSITE: *Stands he, or sits he?*

many occasions, the two become very much interlinked, their practice being parallel activities with one feeding off the other so that the definition between them becomes blurred and they fuse into one activity. This is certainly the ideal, for it is this fusing together that makes for the most effective and rewarding results in terms of understanding the text that is being worked upon.

No playwright's work necessitates and instigates this holistic approach more than William Shakespeare. His work, being that of a genius, blends together aspects of meaning, interpretation, poetry and form in an enthralling mix that entices and engages the practitioner into a harmonious use of all their skills and techniques. Not that this therefore becomes an arduous task, for there is nothing more stimulating and addictive than working upon a Shakespearean text and, as more and more possibilities of supporting the performance with study and illumination and understanding emerge, so does the task become more of a joy and privilege.

If you accept that studying the work of a playwright with a view to performance is to become part of a partnership – a vital relationship within the unique three-way process that includes the audience – then to work with Shakespeare is to work with the very best. Quite contrary to common belief, Shakespeare is not difficult to master. He is challenging without doubt (and this is part of the attraction), but the quality of the work, and the endless open-ended opportunities for researching and analysing in so many different ways, helps and encourages the practitioner in a way no other author can match.

In order to identify and examine the various topics for research and analysis, and how each should be approached, it will be helpful to use a particular Shakespearean speech in order to act as template, example and point of reference. In order that this may be appropriate to both sexes, a speech of chorus has been chosen for this purpose. The Chorus from the play *Henry V* acts within the drama as a narrator: setting the scene, informing the audience of important facts and time transitions and generally encouraging and driving the action. Appearing at the beginning of each of the five acts, and addressing the audience with a prologue to the scenes ahead, each visitation by the Chorus keeps the action flowing and encourages and directs the attention of the onlookers.

Read the speech through very carefully before progressing further with this chapter. Remember the advice given earlier about reading a text initially and give particular attention to the following points.

- Allow yourself to have a reaction to the words. Read them with an open mind and be aware of the images and thoughts that present themselves to you. Try to formulate a general understanding of what the speech is about but do not try to be specific at this stage. Allow it to wash over you and accept the feelings that it promotes in you. Above all, try to see the speech in personal terms – what does it mean to you in particular?
- Begin to hear your 'voice' as if you were performing the speech. Explore with your thoughts the type of character that might emerge if you were playing this particular part. Remember to be broad and unsubtle in

this thinking, so as to liberate possibilities rather than inhibit them.
- Even prior to examining the different areas of research and analysis that this chapter will suggest, start the process by considering part of the speech that you feel would particularly benefit from some exploration; get a feel for any particular lines that seem to promote a sense of analytical reasoning in your head. Ultimately it is you as a practitioner – be it acting or directing – who will need to engage with this speech and therefore your approach to it must be instinctive and personal.

At some stage it will be useful for you to read the whole play, particularly as it is used as an example again later in the book. However, for the time being, a thorough familiarity with the speech in isolation will suffice.

> O for a muse of fire, that
> would ascend
> The brightest heaven of
> invention.
> A kingdom for a stage,
> princess to act,
> And monarchs to behold the
> swelling scene.
> Then should the warlike
> Harry, like himself,
> Assume the port of Mars, and
> at his heels,
> Leashed in like hounds,
> should famine, sword, and
> fire
> Crouch for employment. But
> pardon, gentles all,
> The flat unraised spirits
> that hath dared
> On this unworthy scaffold to
> bring forth
> So great an object. Can this
> cock-pit hold
> The vasty fields of France?

Or may we cram
Within this wooden O the
very casques
That did affright the air At
Agincourt?
O pardon: since a crooked
figure may
Attest in little place a
million,
And let us, ciphers to this
great account,
On your imaginary forces
work.
Suppose within the girdle of
these walls

Are now confined two mighty
monarchies,
Whose high upreared and
abutting fronts
The perilous narrow ocean
parts asunder.
Piece out our imperfections
with your thoughts:
Into a thousand parts divide
one man,
And make imaginary
puissance.
Think, when we talk of
horses, that you see them,
Printing their proud hoofs

O for a muse of fire!

```
i'th' receiving earth;
For 'tis your thoughts that
now must deck our kings,
Carry them here and there,
jumping o'er times,
Turning th'accomplishment of
many years
Into an hourglass — for the
which supply,
Admit me chorus to this
history,
Who Prologue-like your
humble patience pray
Gently to hear, kindly to
judge, our play.
```

Having given yourself some time to really steep yourself in this beautiful speech it is now appropriate for you to get to work on it. Although this chapter is primarily concerned with familiarizing you with the various areas of research and analysis connected to Shakespearean drama, it also provides an ideal opportunity for you to put these into practice for real. Therefore, use the following pointers to actively and thoroughly study the speech and see how much you can discover and evaluate for yourself amongst these relatively few lines. The exercise will not only broaden your abilities but, bearing in mind the subject matter, should also enthuse and stimulate you immeasurably.

WRITING FORM

One of your primary areas of study when encountering the work of Shakespeare will be the various forms of writing that he uses and, in connection with this, the speaking of them and, perhaps most importantly of all, why he uses each different method of writing and when. It is not only important for you to have an understanding of the mechanics of his writing, and the translation of them into speech and acting, but also of the significance of their use and their contribution to the artistic and dramatic purposes of the works.

The example speech is common to much of Shakespearean text in as much as it is written in Shakespeare's principal writing style, that of blank verse constructed of iambic pentameter. The verse is 'blank' because it has no particular rhyming devices and, as a general rule (although there are exceptions), each line is made-up of five metrical feet (poetic forms of musical bars) with each foot being comprised of two beats (or syllables) with the first of the two unstressed and the second stressed – 'de-dum'.

The other two main forms of Shakespeare's writing are rhyming couplets (pairs of lines with endings that rhyme with each other) and prose (standard writing using normal sentence construction and punctuation).

Shakespeare tends to use iambic pentameter for the more elaborately based, dramatic, rhetorical, poetic literary expressive scenes and characters; rhyming couplets for romantic lovers and flowery platitudes; while prose is reserved for the more down-to-earth, basic and matter-of-fact scenarios and people. The play *A Midsummer Night's Dream* provides an excellent example of this usage as it contains all three forms in typical deployment. Of particular note is the blank versification of the fairies and courtly human characters, while the working-class and simple 'Rude Mechanicals' speak in good solid prose. A detailed reading of this play will not only acquaint you with the writing forms but also develop a personal understanding of their significance and the parallel that exists between them and Shakespearean acting and characterization.

It is part of the genius of Shakespeare that any research and analysis of his work must embrace the very writing form itself, and it is truly inspiring that, obtaining an understanding of the stories and the characters that people them, includes an appreciation of the very words themselves and the technicality of their writing.

You should now look again at the example speech and view it from the perspective of its verse form. While the characterization and rendition of the speech is very much a question of personal interpretation, there is a strong lead given in the way in which it is written as to the potential manifestation of both. As with all great drama, interpretation by actor and director is fundamental to the process, but here you will find yet another aspect for potential study that will inform, enable and educate that interpretation.

In addition to this, and without doubt, this speech of the Chorus is made extraordinarily beautiful by the use of its wonderfully free-flowing and expressive verse form. However, it is not the form itself but the mastery and excellence of it that is responsible for this. Part of your study of this, and all other Shakespearean text, should be angled towards gaining an appreciation of a personal analysis of its quality. For going hand in hand with its poetic greatness is its facility for leading a theatre practitioner confidently and knowledgeably towards making the right acting and production decisions.

There are many books that will cover the subject of Shakespearean verse forms and writing style. In particular, you should aim for those written from practical experience – actors and directors – for the relevance here for you, as with most of your study, is highly weighted towards application of knowledge rather than an academic appreciation of it.

VOICE AND SPEECH

With a playwright of such literary ability, and verse and writing forms of such complexity, it becomes obvious that a particular emphasis must be placed upon an acquisition of the vocal technical expertise required to do justice to it. As the research and analysis dealt with within this book is geared towards the practical application of text within theatrical production, an understanding of the relationship between the text and the techniques needed to bring it alive is essential. Therefore, part of your research effort must be invested in an investigation of technical ability and its facilitation.

The verse contained within the example speech is particularly demanding upon all aspects of voice and speech, with articulation, breath control and dexterity all being of major importance. The very rhythm of the verse necessitates an insurance to not break or distort lines in an uncontrolled or inappropriate way. However, it should not be thought that Shakespearean verse is brittle, delicate or temperamental: this is far from the truth as the lines mould themselves towards the actor's use of variety of speech in terms of pace, pause, pitch, volume and phrasing with surprising pliability. The quality of their construction makes them extremely 'user-friendly', not the reverse. It is the need for the actor to control the speaking of these lines that throws so much emphasis upon the technical dexterity and capability of their speaking.

While the rhythmic construction of the verse will allow itself to be pulled, drawn, extended and foreshortened at will, it will also, by means of compensation, require the knowledge and ability for this to be balanced elsewhere in order to preserve the fluidity of the metre. For instance, if a pause is taken (and perhaps stretched out) early in a line, it will usually require an acceleration of pace later in the line in order to earn its existence. This will require technical agility as well as theoretical experience and knowledge.

In the same way, pausing and the associated taking of breath must be born of conscious decision and not technical necessity. Breath control enables an actor to breathe at points in

the verse that will maintain the rhythmical structure and not just when physically unavoidable: a breath taken in the wrong place, and without control, can destroy the metre and also the very sense of the verse. Also, breath that becomes prematurely exhausted towards the end of any given line can cause lack of clarity and even audibility as a 'dropped ending' is created.

An actor's ability to breathe deeply, and to then expel this breath with control, will also allow the voice to possess the power and resonance required when speaking Shakespeare. Beautiful words require a beautiful voice with which to speak them. There is certainly beauty in every human voice but theatre actors must work upon their voices so that this beauty can be liberated and work to its full potential. Directors too must be aware of this, particularly in terms of Shakespeare and other classical texts for, while an actor's technique is primarily their own

Voice is important.

responsibility, an understanding of the part it plays in the production process will be invaluable as a directorial tool.

Another look at the Chorus from the point of view of speech will reveal just how important clarity of diction is in its execution. It contains elaborate words, densely packed and ingeniously juxtaposed. This will require an actor to match the quality of the writing with the dexterity and precision of vocal prowess. It is a sobering thought that in this, and so many other areas, the greatest playwright (perhaps writer) of all time is totally dependent upon the many workaday practitioners who interpret his work. In this instance a simple thing such as sloppy diction can totally halt the genius in his tracks and prevent his magnificent muse from reaching its intended target – the audience.

Vocal Practice

In order to practise both breath control and diction, speak the following short speech from *Twelfth Night*, making sure that you breathe deeply, control the outward breath (using it to fully support the voice to the end of each line) and shape each word clearly and sharply. Do not view this simply as a technical exercise, but colour the language with your own personal interpretation of what is being said.

```
If music be the food of love,
play on;
Give me excess of it, that,
surfeiting,
The appetite may sicken, and so
die.
That strain again! It had a
dieing fall:
O! it came o'er my ear like the
sweet sound
That breathes upon a bank of
violets,
Stealing and giving odour.
Enough! No more:
'Tis not so sweet now as it was
before.
O spirit of love! How quick and
fresh art thou,
That, not withstanding thy
capacity
Receiveth as the sea, nought
enters there,
Of what validity and pitch
soe'er,
But falls into abatement and low
price,
Even in a minute: so full of
shapes is fancy,
That it alone is high
fantastical.
```

If music be the food of love, play on.

Your research in terms of voice and speech should be very much within a practical framework. Search out books and other sources that will give you a working knowledge of voice: look in particular at the areas of voice production, breath control and the strengthening of articulation. Also, find an appropriate class and join it; for voice is a subject that must be studied for real rather than just read about or mused upon.

WRITING OF THE UNUSUAL

One of the most significant factors that leads to the illusion that Shakespeare is difficult to understand (perhaps even incomprehensible to some) is the way he sometimes expresses ideas, sentiments and facts, that are in themselves perfectly simple and straightforward, but

that a modern reader can find unusual and unfamiliar. He will very often reverse two elements of a sentence or phrase, or construct his phraseology using elements of grammar and vocabulary that are seemingly out of the ordinary, suspect or even plain incorrect.

Then should the warlike Harry, like himself ...

It is necessary for the student of Shakespeare to be aware of these and include their

86

unravelling within their research and analysis criteria. This is not only for the purpose of making the meaning clear so that it can be properly acted and communicated, but also to reveal the beauty of expression that results from this unique manner of writing. Therefore, you should not think of these manifestations as irritants to your work but as the very stuff of your reason for working upon the texts in the first place.

A wonderful example of this from the speech is: *Then should the warlike Harry, like himself, Assume the port of Mars.* It is the short parenthesis, *like himself,* that is of particular interest here. The rest of the two-line phrase of thought is relatively clear and straightforward: King Henry (Harry) would become like the God of War (Mars). When placed in context with the lines before, this makes even more sense as it becomes apparent that the Chorus is telling the audience that Henry would appear this way if he (*the Chorus*) and his fellow actors inhabited a better and more worthy theatrical environment in which to tell the story (*A kingdom for a stage, princess to act, And monarchs to behold the swelling scene*).

However, the *like himself,* while seamlessly integrating itself rhythmically within the verse, is at first sight confusing and is unnecessary; it almost breaks the sense, but given a second look it becomes apparent that, far from detracting from the meaning, it adds to it in a quite brilliantly economic way. This simple pair of words, consisting only of three syllables, confirm the main thrust of the thought: Henry would be seen as he is, as he should be and in perfect portrayal: *like himself.* The audience is not only being informed that this great king deserves better representation but that without it he is diminished and embodied in a way that defies the reality – the fact is better than the available quality of the fiction.

This is a wonderful example of how Shakespearean poetry can speak with such a succinct and perfect voice, making many layered statements but making them effortlessly and with clarity. If you try to write the same idea using your own prose it will become clear just how inadequate alternative words to Shakespeare's become when compared to his own. For example:

If we had a good enough theatre Harry would seem like a God because that is what he really is.

Given facilities worthy of the subject, the subject would appear as worthy as it should be.

Henry is so great he is like the God of War and that is how he should be portrayed, but the actors, theatre and audience are not adequate to such a task.

Although such attempts to replicate the meaning of the lines are clumsy and almost comic by comparison, they serve more than the purpose of highlighting Shakespeare's great talent. By doing this, the practitioner can confirm for themselves that they are cognizant of exactly what they will be saying when they speak the lines in performance. The beauty and poetic brilliance of the words will look after themselves, but the correct thought process, giving them substance and clarity, is the responsibility of the actor in collaboration with his or her director. Therefore the process of research and analysis into this, and other similar constructions within the texts, is absolutely vital and one of your foremost responsibilities as a practitioner of Shakespeare and his fellows.

Some reading connected to Shakespeare's use of language may be useful to you, but do not wade in too deep, as it is not necessary for you to become academically expert in this area – just aware and responsive to his thinking and expression.

The 'Thee and Thou' Syndrome

It is well worth dispelling another popular myth at this point in the shape of the commonly held theory that Shakespeare's plays are written in Old English. This is not true and historically ignorant. In fact, the English used by Shakespeare is recognizably modern in many parts but, as already stated, it is language often couched in unfamiliar terms and is also densely packed with poetic and artistically elaborate expression. The often-occurring use of 'old-fashioned' terms such as *Thee*, *Thou*, *Sire* and *Anon* and so on can also cause much bewilderment, especially amongst the young. It would be sacrilege to desire to alter the idiosyncratic style of Shakespeare, as therein lies much of his appeal and a good deal of his genius, but it is your job and responsibility to unravel this rich tapestry of language in terms of thought processes so that the beauty of expression can be fully realized in recognizable meaning.

It should not matter a jot if a reader of Shakespeare is confused and irritated by what may seem to them as outdated, complex and overblown literary elitism, nor if they struggle to see through the density of language to the truth beneath. However, if an audience receiving your performance is equally inclined to such reaction (for to watch a play is the principal manner in which to experience it, hence your part in the process) then something has gone very wrong. Of course an audience should be aware of the beauty, richness and colour of the language, but they should also be able to effortlessly allow this greatness of writing to communicate its meaning directly and unambiguously.

It must never be forgotten that the major factor determining Shakespeare's success and durability down the years is his ability to speak directly to audiences of all ages and at different times, and this is achieved by his plain, straightforward portrayal of human existence, frailty and triumph – a mirror of life held up to all to be plainly seen. This must work because of the way the plays are written, not despite it; most importantly, if an audience is allowed to become alienated by the text it will fail completely. Therefore, the importance of your study in terms of discovering the 'modern' within the 'old-fashioned', the 'simple' within the 'complex' and the 'truth' within the 'poetry' cannot be overestimated.

Here then is another area where you must sieve the text in order to identify areas that need your clarification in terms of meaning. You should be aware that this is not just a case of looking up words and simply determining their theoretical definitions, nor of being able to substitute new for old words in your head; a good actor (aided by a good director) should know why a word or phrase is being said in practical terms; the context and not just the reason; the intention and not just the meaning. For instance, when saying *thou*, in any particular situation (quite apart from meaning 'you'), the question should be asked as to what lies behind the use of the word – is there emotion attached? In a modern play an actor would be ready and able to place an emotional context in the word 'you', for instance, in the line '*you* were the person who reported me to the police'. Just because Shakespeare uses 'Thou' instead of 'you' does not mean that these four letters are any less deserving of interpretation as well as clear meaning. Unfamiliar words must be acted and not just translated; in this way, an audience will have no problem with them even if they have never spoken or even heard them before.

Unfortunately the Chorus speech does not really contain examples of these curios, except perhaps the word '*tis*, which is really more suited to examination in another context later in this chapter.

Shakespearean Exclamation

However, there are examples in the example speech of a very important but much overlooked feature of Shakespearean text, that of the appearance and clever use of exclamation. Here we find it in the sound O, as in: *O for a Muse of fire* and *O pardon!* This again can cause problems for the young actor as, because it is 'Shakespeare' they fail to identify his exclamations in the same way as they would modern ones, that they use frequently.

As example: an actor will often over-pronounce an exclamation such as O in a way they would never do in, say, the modern-usage expression *Oh, I'm fed up!* In a line such as this, the exclamation ('oh') is simply an aside, a jumping off point for the rest of the sentence – hardly of importance as a word but still deeply significant as an exclamation. It does not necessarily though have to be thrown away in delivery and could, of course, be stressed to accentuate the sentiment to come, such as being drawn out like *'ohhhhhhh, I am fed up'*. None the less, it is an exclamation and will always be treated as one (with an important part to play – no more, no less), while the Shakespearean O (and indeed many other of his exclamations) is often given 'word' status and pronounced and emphasized unnaturally and without normal weighting.

Thus, here again, your diligent study of the text comes into play. You must find the thought processes behind these exclamations so that they can be sounded naturally and without an artificial delivery. The best way to approach this is to think more about *why* you are making a sound than about the sound itself.

Reference again to the speech will help enormously with your practice of this. Look again at the first line: *O for a muse of fire*. You will be considering the research and analysis later in this chapter but for the time being imagine yourself an actor with the task of playing this part and decide how you might want to start this speech and the effect that you might wish to create.

Do you want to wander on and begin talking casually to the audience, as if you were engaging them in a casual conversation with the aim of making your points in a relaxed and chatty way? Or would you like to grab their attention forcefully and dramatically by bursting upon them and energetically, enthusiastically and passionately regale them with your personality and dynamic purpose? Either of these choices, or one of many other possibilities, will dictate a very different use of the exclamation in terms of, not necessarily how it is spoken, but how it is used intentionally and dramatically, how it is 'thought'. In truth, the sounds you make will be automatic, but an automation driven and inspired by your thought process, even in relation to this one simple, single-syllable sound.

Missing Syllables

An examination of this speech (and most other Shakespearean writing) will reveal some strange, and sometimes confusing, 'shortenings' of words. For instance: *jumping o'er times*, the *o'er* being the shortening in question. This is yet another small detail that can be disproportionately confusing and a modern actor may find them awkward to speak.

Their origin is linked to the verse structure. They are employed in order to drop one syllable (or beat) and thus keep the rhythmical format of the line. In other words, it maintains ten beats within the line instead of eleven, and so preserves the iambic pentameter.

A clear example of this can be examined in the line *Carry them here and there, jumping o'er times*: the shortening of 'over' to *o'er* does the job and maintains a perfect rhythm for the line. In order to feel this, speak the words as written in the text out loud and allow yourself to gently accentuate the iambic formula. The unhindered flow and easy musicality of

89

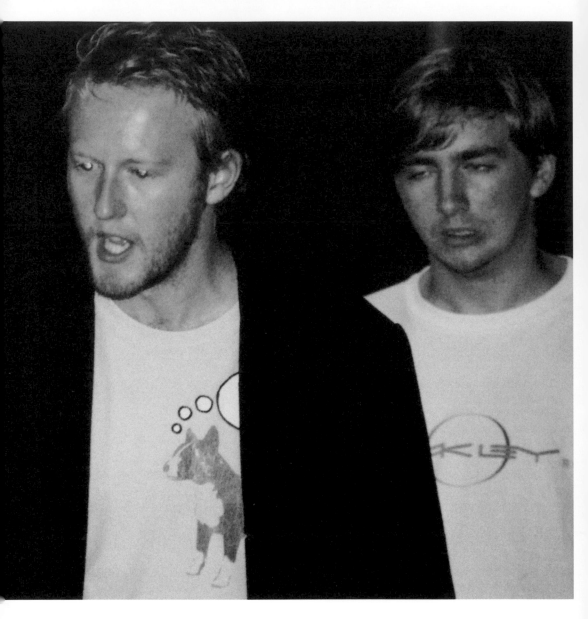

the line should become immediately apparent. Now repeat the process but substitute 'over' for *o'er*. You will soon realize how jarring and awkward the line has become, now quite devoid of its rhythm and pleasing metre.

'Tis your thoughts now shall deck our kings.

The same experiment may be repeated with the line: *Printing their proud hoofs i'the' receiving earth.* Here you will find the shortening of 'in

HISTORICAL FACT

Shakespeare is a very interesting playwright to examine in terms of historical detail. There is, of course, a large collection of his output that falls under the category of 'The History Plays', of which *Henry V* is an important member. However, the historical accuracy of these works should not be taken for granted. Shakespeare was not essentially an historian; neither were his plays written as academic reference works to the periods of history they variously covered. Shakespeare's general source may often have been historical event, themes and figures, but his trade was providing entertainment and dramatic art that owes no automatic dues to factual detail.

Another very important factor to bear in mind is Shakespeare's propensity to portray history in a way that would be palatable to his lords and masters, particularly King James and Queen Elizabeth. Therefore, his view of the past would often be richly coloured by the necessities of the present, and thus could be extremely suspect in terms of accuracy and truth.

It is important that you bear this in mind when researching and, in particular, analysing historical fact and its purpose within the play you are studying. While an actor playing Richard The Third would rightly be concerned with developing the character as presented by Shakespeare (in all his evil, scheming glory), it would be appropriate and useful for that actor to be aware of the relationship between Shakespeare's fiction and history's fact and to possess the extra, and somewhat contradictory knowledge, afforded by a little independent research. The resulting analysis of Shakespeare's monster and the man of history will arm the actor with more layers of source material upon which to build characterization. A director, having studied as widely, would be equally empowered by this additional depth of information, thus enriching the production and informing the interpretation.

A Point about Preservation

When studying Shakespearean texts it is important to realize that the plays were not actually published until after Shakespeare's death. Therefore, it may be reasonably assumed that many of the peculiarities of line and word construction will derive from the difficult process of gathering the texts together as accurately as possible from varied and widespread sources so long after they were first written.

In some cases, it can be observed that certain lines are short and do not fill the full iambic pentameter line. In such instances, the first word will start late in the line with no text before it. This may be because the compiler was uncertain as to what the rest of the line should be (it may have been missing completely) and therefore left a blank as an obvious place of academic omission.

It should also be remembered that, as the texts have been printed and reprinted over the years, various inaccuracies may have been compounded and it is unlikely that the plays remain as accurate as when they were first written and performed.

---

the' has the same effect and produces a marvellous musicality to the line. This line is particularly interesting in the fact that the *i'the'* spans the end of one metrical foot (group of two beats) and the start of the next. However, it works in just the same way, as does the previously *'tis* in the line *For 'tis your thoughts that now must deck our kings.*

These idiosyncrasies of Shakespearean verse are more than worthy of your study as they are so much a part of the equation in terms of verse speaking and, as you become familiar with them and their usage, you will find the way that they punctuate and enable the verse to be of help rather than hindrance.

The main aspects of historical research prompted by the Chorus speech are that of King Henry V as a man in general and of the Battle of Agincourt in particular. This campaign is very relevant to the character of Henry. This was a battle of particular pertinence to his emotional journey throughout the play. The English were heavily outnumbered and the endeavour was seemingly of dubious wisdom. Couple this with the play's depiction of Henry's need to prove himself as a great leader of men and a worthy king, and there immediately emerges the kind of tension between character and situation that drives much good drama and provides a perfect entrée into the character's thematic purpose for the actor. Here again you witness research meeting analysis to form interpretation.

In parallel to these main points and in terms of a slightly different historical subject matter, but equally important and very relevant to men and women of the theatre, is the reference to Shakespeare Theatre itself:

> But pardon, gentles all,
> The flat unraised spirits
> that hath dared
> On this unworthy scaffold to
> bring forth
> So great an object. Can this
> cock-pit hold
> The vasty fields of France?
> Or may we cram
> Within this wooden O the
> very casques
> That did affright the air At
> Agincourt?

Interesting here is the way in which Shakespeare belittles the arena in which he works in favour of the magnificence of his subject matter. This in itself can act as a sobering and prioritizing warning to some of the architectural elaborations (and in some case abominations),

along with a propensity to lavish production values, that have dominated much of theatre down the years. Shakespeare is very firmly telling us that it is the play that is important, not the theatrical trappings that attend it – a useful piece of analysis indeed!

Despite its relevance to this speech and the play from which it derives, a knowledge of Shakespeare's Globe Theatre (*this wooden O*) should be essential to all theatre practitioners: not just in terms of the physical geography of the building but also in relation to the way in which the plays were staged there and the manner and style of their presentation. There are, of course, many books that will provide all of this information in detail but, in this area of research, there is a unique opportunity to experience something close to the real thing in the shape of a living, working museum: the re-created Globe Theatre in London. If your time, budget and residential location allow you the opportunity of visiting here, you should certainly make the effort to do so. Not only will you be able to see a life-size replica of the Theatre in three-dimensional accuracy, but watching a production there, will give you a feel for Shakespeare's original productions in a way quite unavailable anywhere else.

There is an added reason why this topic is important in relation to this particular speech and it bears direct relation to the actual circumstances of a production at the original Globe Theatre. Many of the audience members for the first production of *Henry V* would, as for the other productions, be standing in the main open ground area of the Theatre and were known as 'The Groundlings'. Unlike in modern theatres, these patrons would not have paid to enter the arena. Instead, their money would be collected while they were in there by a man who would circulate amongst them, collecting the company's remunerations as fast and as effectively as he could. This person was called 'the Gatherer', for obvious reasons. A

A Practical Recap

Consider the following speech of Cleopatra's in terms of all the various points of research and analysis mentioned in this chapter. Think of as many avenues of interpretational study as you can and consider your reaction to performing or directing it.

As well as containing many pertinent points to work upon, it contains some beautiful imagery to unravel and interpret.

O, Charmian,
Where think'st thou he is now?
Stands he, or sits he?
Or does he walk? Or is he on his horse?
O happy horse, to bear the weight of Antony!
Do bravely, horse, for wot'st thou whom thou mov'st?
The demi-Atlas of this earth, the arm
And burgonet of men. He's speaking now,
Or murmuring 'Where's my serpent of old Nile?'
For so he calls me. Now I feed myself
With most delicious poison.
Think on me,
That am with Phoebus' amorous pinches black
And wrinkled deep in time.
Broad-fronted Caesar,
When thou wast here above the ground, I was
A morsel for a monarch; and great Pompey
Would stand and make his eyes grow in my brow;
There would he anchor his aspect, and die
With looking on his life.

groundling would probably try to avoid paying this fee until he or she had established whether or not the play was likely to be worth watching in its entirety. Thus, they would try to avoid 'The Gatherer' as long as possible and slip out without paying if the production was not perceived to be sufficiently absorbing.

Considering the fact that this was very much a commercial enterprise, with a hand-to-mouth necessity to keep a steady level of income, the actor playing the Chorus, with the lonely task of starting the play, may very well have felt considerable pressure to grab the audience's attention quickly and irrevocably. This is not only of interest to the would-be re-creator of this role but yet another contributory source of information for the formulation of characterization and playing style.

A secondary but still useful point of research in this speech may be prompted by the phrase: *Assume the port of Mars.* Of course Shakespeare here is using this reference in an historical context himself but, as it is used as a metaphor for such great power and spectacle, it cannot be anything but useful to have a knowledge of this Roman god, his allegorical reputation throughout history and, in particular, how an audience of Shakespeare's time would view this as a dramatic allusion.

With time to spare, it may well be worth examining the details of a battle in this period. The Chorus is keen to tell the audience that, given better facilities, the theatre company would dearly love to convey the confrontation between the English and French (*two mighty monarchies*) with exciting and colourful splendour: *Think, when we talk of horses, that you see them, printing their proud hoofs i'th' receiving earth*). Therefore, it will be interesting to know just how this would have looked, sounded and felt in reality.

In the case of Shakespeare there is no detail too small that is not worthy of investigation; mindful, of course, of a careful budgeting and prioritizing of time.

7 KNOWING THE CHARACTERS (IN THEORY)

THE RIGHT ATTITUDE TO CHARACTER

As drama is usually concerned with some kind of conflict (in all its various forms), and because a play may often take a particular moral standpoint (in terms of a political, religious or philosophical agenda), it is often a perceivable factor within the narrative that a character is 'good or bad', 'right or wrong', 'sympathetic or unsympathetic'. Both directors and actors must remember that this is a perception that a playwright may well be encouraging an audience to make, but it is not advisable to predetermine the same judgements in terms of the interpretation of the text. Theatre practitioners must be focused upon why characters act in certain ways; what their motivations are; how they personally justify these factors. For them there should be no such thing as playing the 'goody' or the 'baddy' (except perhaps in pantomime), but of determining and portraying the truth of what a character is and does and the reality of their lives that leads them to the choices that they make.

The Journey

It should be established early on in your examination of character that a playwright does not people a play haphazardly but with the specific agenda of enabling the story to be accurately

OPPOSITE: A character's journey begins.

> ### Jumping in at the Deep End
>
> In order to kick-start your understanding of a text in terms of character, ask yourself the following questions about any particular role you are studying.
>
> - What is my character like and how do they behave?
> - What do they seem to want to achieve?
> - What are their strengths and weaknesses?
> - What influences them?
> - What is their environment like?
> - What opportunities do they have and what constrains them?
> - What are the physical realities of their daily lives: housing, clothing, diet and so on?
>
> Keep the list in mind as you consider the various sections of this chapter.

told and the focus and intentions of the play properly realized. Because of this, we find upon the pages of the text characterizations that may well be colourfully and expertly drawn, but always in respect of what the play is about and the journey that each character has to make within it. You will, of course, want to bring full life to these characters, so that they are believable as entities both within and without the context of the play's particular plot.

However, you have nothing to work with but the 'slice' of life that is relevant to each character within the limitations of what actually happens to them during the course of the story. It will be hoped that your imagination and talent will broaden and enhance this, but your source material remains specific to the work's particular story and purpose. Therefore it is with this that you must begin your work and there is no better framework for your analysis than the 'journey' just mentioned. So, as you continue with this chapter, you will be using this analogy upon which to base and structure your character work.

The Starting Place

The journey that a character takes during a play is, of course, a 'life' journey and not a geographical one (although, in some cases, this may apply too): it will be a journey of understanding, of change, of spiritual development, of emotional upheaval or a combination of these, and other, factors.

The 'starting place' for any character's journey within the play is not the 'starting place' for the journey of their lives so, as you begin working on a play, you should be concerned with establishing at what point of their life development they find themselves as the curtain rises.

Therefore it will be helpful to ask yourself three more similar (but slightly more specific) questions for any given character in connection with the start of the play and in specific relation to their impending 'journey':

1. *What are the physical and emotional circumstances of their lives?*
2. *What motivates their behaviour?*
3. *What are their ambitions and priorities for the future?*

Although each of these questions may be looked at individually, the answers to them will be dependent on one important factor: past history. In life, a person is the product of what has happened to them in the past both in general terms (for instance the nature of their upbringing) and specific terms (such as particular life-moulding experiences); so it is for fictitious characters in drama.

In light of this, you should begin by investigating a character's 'past history' very thoroughly. There will be two sources for this:

1. *Information that is given to you directly by the playwright.*
2. *Information that you must assume or imagine.*

However, you will see that these two sources are not unconnected and that the second point is inevitably reliant upon the first. The playwright, either by way of a stage direction or within the narrative, may tell you that a character suffered badly in the past during, say, the Second World War. However, even if you were not told this, you might well assume it if you were simply given the certain information, that the play was set in 1960, that the character was fifty years old and by nationality a German Jew. This is obviously a very broad example but it should make the point that given information a theatre practitioner's creative judgement must work hand in hand with this information in order to create the reality required by the text.

Do not underestimate your own contribution in this. Neither should you feel prohibited from making decisions about your character that seem pertinent to you and that are not contradicted by the script. For instance, just because a play is set in Britain and there is absolutely no mention of a character's nationality of origin you do not need to assume that they are necessarily British. If it suits the other factors of interpretation you have made, both factually and imaginatively, to consider them to be of a particular foreign origin, then you are perfectly entitled to do

Past History in Practice

In terms of establishing the past history of a character, both in terms of information readily available within the play and that needing to be creatively imagined or interpreted, the following pointers will serve to start the process.

- *When were they born?*
- *Where?*
- *What were the circumstances of their childhood?*
- *What was their education?*
- *What have been the details of their working lives?*
- *What have been the details of their emotional lives?*
- *What has brought them to this 'place' at the start of the play?*
- *Do they want to be here or not – and why?*

Henry V is a play that concerns itself with the young prince's journey from boyhood to manhood, as he becomes king and takes on, amongst other things, his country's mantle against the French. His past history, so clearly documented in the previous play in the cycle, dictates a starting place for this character that is wholly indicative of one of the play's major themes. Hal, faced with inheriting the most responsible and arduous job imaginable, does so firmly under the gaze of a sceptical and suspicious populace, all wondering how the country's fortunes will fare under the influence of one so renown for his riotous lifestyle and less than responsible demeanour.

The journey continues.

so. This is all part of the unique partnership between you and the author, between the text and interpretation of the text.

Now it will help you to consider a practical example of a real play in terms of establishing a particular understanding of its leading character's 'starting place' by an identification and interpretation of their 'past history'. Shakespeare's *Henry V* is a somewhat fascinatingly unusual choice of example in this respect, as a complete research of its eponymous hero's past history can be obtained in another play, *Henry IV Part Two*; this plays resides in a sequence between *Henry IV Part One* and *Henry V*. In it we can observe the young Prince Hal (later to become King Henry V) as a young, fun-loving tearaway, dedicated to enjoying his youth and carousing his days away in the company of a less than seemly crew of rough-and-ready companions.

The Journey to Come

It is Hal's reaction to this challenge that galvanizes the play into a wonderful execution of its patriotic and heroic themes. Determined to put his past behind him and prove himself to his people as a strong and dependable leader (and man), he reveals a growing strength of character and purpose and begins to execute his kingly role with magnificent power and eloquence.

The following speech underlines this impressive flowering of regal maturity as, under extreme pressure and with many expectant gazes turned upon him, the new King Henry V brilliantly responds and ripostes with total control and dignity to a grossly insulting message sent from France, even managing a kingly courtesy and plenty of ready wit.

> We are glad the Dauphin is
> so pleasant with us.
> His present, and your pains,
> we thank you for.
> When we have matched our
> rackets to these balls,
> We will in France, by God's
> Grace, play a set
> Shall strike his father's
> crown into the hazard.
> Tell him he hath made a
> match with such a wrangler
> That all the courts of
> France will be disturbed
> With chases. And we
> understand him well,
> How he comes o'er us with
> our wilder days,
> Not measuring what use we
> made of them.
> We never valued this poor
> seat of England,
> And therefore, living hence,
> did give ourself
> To barbarous licence; as
> 'tis ever common

> That men are merriest when
> they are from home.
> But tell the Dauphin I will
> keep my state,
> Be like a king, and show my
> sale of greatness,
> When I do rouse me in my
> throne of France.
> For that I have laid by my
> majesty,
> And plodded like a man for
> working-days;
> But I will rise there with
> so full a glory
> That I will dazzle all the
> eyes of France,
> Yea, strike the Dauphin
> blind to look on us.
> And tell the pleasant Prince
> this mock of his
> Hath turned his balls to
> gun-stones, and his soul
> Shall stand sore charged for
> the wasteful vengeance
> That shall fly with them:
> for many a thousand widows
> Shall this his mock mock out
> of their dear husbands;
> Mock mothers from their
> sons, mock castles down;
> And some are yet ungotten
> and unborn
> That shall have cause to
> curse the Dauphin's scorn.
> But this lies all within the
> will of God,
> To whom I do appeal, and in
> whose name,
> Tell you the Dauphin, I am
> coming on,
> To venge me as I may, and to
> put forth
> My rightful hand in a well-
> hallowed cause.

```
So get you hence in peace;
and tell the Dauphin
His jest will savour but of
shallow wit
When thousands weep more
than did laugh at it.
Convey them with safe
conduct. Fare you well.
```

There is much to research and analyse here generally, as the speech is steeped in references, allusions, word play, metaphors and theatrical devices, as well as containing a huge amount of relevant and significant information in terms of the plot, characterization, themes and overall purposes of this great play.

In terms of particular concern to the emphasis of this chapter, the actor's main analysis of this speech should not just be primarily focused upon the power, dominance, brutal self-honesty and gallant defiance of it, but upon the huge, underlying responsibility that the character is feeling for its successful execution and the significant turning point it represents in his journey. It is very much a building block upon which the future development of the character will be constructed.

Upon the Journey

However, this starting place as discussed also determines an element within the play and its themes that explores a more personal and human aspect of his impending journey; for there is a price to pay for his transformation and it is that of his isolation from, and consequent rejection of, his former friends. This underlines the constantly occurring focus of research and interpretation upon the significances of the human existence. Any actor playing Henry V will not only find his starting place informing him of his journey towards power and glory, but also of another (more rigorous) journey through the emotional twists and turns of his thoughts and feelings. In this,

highly contrasting speech from later in the play, it can be witnessed just how high a price Henry has had to pay in terms of his isolation, sense of responsibility and loneliness. It is possible almost to feel his anger, desperation and isolation in this beautiful soliloquy.

```
Upon the King.
'Let us our lives, our
souls, our debts, our care-
full
wives,
Our children, and our sins,
lay on the King.'
We must bear all. O hard
condition,
Twin-born with greatness,
subject to the breath
Of every fool whose sense no
more can feel
But his own wringing. What
infinite heart's ease
Must kings neglect that pri-
vate men enjoy?
And what have kings that
privates have not too,
Save ceremony, save general
ceremony?
And what art thou, thou idol
Ceremony?
What kind of god art thou,
that suffer'st more
Of mortal griefs than do thy
worshippers?
What are thy rents? What are
thy comings-in?
O Ceremony, show me but thy
worth!
What is thy soul of adora-
tion?
Art thou aught else but
place, degree, and form,
Creating awe and fear in
other men?
```

```
Wherein thou art less happy,
being feared,
Than they in fearing.
What drink'st thou oft,
instead of homage sweet,
But poisoned flattery?
O be sick, great greatness,
And bid thy Ceremony give
thee cure!
```

```
Prepare we for our marriage;
on which day,
My Lord of Burgundy, we'll
take our oath,
And all the peers', for
surety of our leagues.
Then shall O swear to Kate,
and you to me,
And may our oaths well Kept
and prosperous be!
```

This speech is a direct development of the research and analysis resulting from the previous play and analyses the highly emotional nature of character development within good drama. A huge amount of understanding must be established by the actor for his or her character at the start of any play and much of this will be achieved by simple applied research. However, what grows from it is the subsequent realization of a feeling, thinking person, uniquely bound up with the actor's own emotional capabilities and empathies with the human condition. The speech in this case serves as a wonderful example of how a scene (properly established by what has occurred before in the play) can hold up a mirror to the soul of a character as determined by the playwright in harmony with the actor.

Henry completes his 'journey' (as does the actor playing him) by successfully mastering all of the personal and professional challenges that the play (and perhaps history) has set him and finds fulfilment, happiness and the culmination of his ambition and purpose in his marriage to Princess Katherine of France. It is significant that even his last words of happiness and conclusion in the play are highly resonant with the feelings of honour and statesmanship. It should be noted from this that even though a character journeys in terms of personal development and circumstance throughout a play, the core values and preoccupations of that character will usually remain constant and relevant.

Research and Character

Ask yourself the following questions about any particular piece of research with regard to character.

- How does this factor affect the living conditions of the characters in the play?
- How does this factor affect the physical practicalities of their daily lives: housing, clothing, diet, and so on?
- How does this factor affect the behaviour of the characters?
- How does this factor influence the choices they make?
- How does this factor affect their personalities?
- How does this factor affect their opportunities and constraint?
- How does this factor affect their outlook on life?
- How does this factor affect the tensions and conflicts within the play?

Another example of a great play (moving swiftly forwards in time of writing) will highlight a very different starting place for a character, an equally different method of determining it and a very different kind of journey.

In George Bernard Shaw's *Pygmalion*, the character of Eliza begins her sojourn as a poor downtrodden flower girl, living close to poverty and possessing not only the manner and speech of a typical girl of her class but all of the social disadvantage and prejudice that attend it.

The direct source of research in terms of understanding the character's situation at this starting point will be very much based upon historical background and, parallel to this, the social conventions of the time. It will be necessary for the actor to gain an understanding not only of Eliza's likely circumstances but of the juxtaposition between her class and those above her and the social 'glue' that maintained the status quo. This is not only potentially fascinating research but highly relevant to the themes and intentions of the author. In relation to this, it will be useful to consider certain points that will have a bearing upon the character's journey to come.

- George Bernard Shaw was very much concerned in his writing about social inequality and political change. This in itself is a factor that could potentially not only be discovered by research, but could also be the source of obtaining greater understanding of his work by further study of this aspect of his writing. It is not difficult to deduce from these factors concerning the author that Eliza's journey will not be without relevance to his preoccupations as a writer.
- Although Eliza is very much a working-class girl, with a woeful lack of education, she is highly intelligent. This should become apparent to the actor playing her from

only a little study of the part and it is extremely relevant in that her journey is likely to be one driven by self-motivation, ambition and determination, rather than just drifting upon a tide of circumstance. As the play develops it is likely that the character will systematically begin to exert control over her chaotic environment.

Having thought briefly about character in theory, it will now be necessary for you to begin the practice of understanding text in terms of characterization in practice.

Journey's end.

8 KNOWING THE CHARACTERS (IN PRACTICE)

LIVING RESEARCH AND ANALYSIS

Having researched and analysed character from a somewhat academic point of view – the facts about their lives, the circumstances of their living conditions, their past history and the parochial and dramatic factors that shape their journey throughout the play – it is now time to examine the process of using this information to create characters that live and breathe upon the stage; to find a physical representation for your labours and to be able to ensure that your study results in a believable and sympathetic persona that inhabits the environment of the play naturally, spontaneously and, above all, truthfully.

In order to focus upon this very practical process it will be more appropriate, and less confusing, to concentrate upon the actor rather than the director here; for while the theoretical research of character is common to both, this more practical application of analytical skill is, by its very nature, only directly applicable to the actor. However, how an actor approaches these endeavours is still of great relevance to the director in terms of his or her core function of 'enabling' actors to do their work properly, and so the following

OPPOSITE: An actor must believe in the character he or she is playing.

will still be of great relevance to them even though not directly from their own particular perspective.

Much of the theoretical side of research (and, to a certain extent, analysis) is ideally conducted prior to the rehearsal period, although not all, as the complete process will need to be informed by the communal experience of working on a play with others and sharing their insights and visions for the work. However, the practical application of an actor's skills will be naturally more focused within the rehearsals themselves and, with this in mind, it will be helpful to examine them in the context of rehearsing and the progressive nature of finding and building a character bit by bit and from one rehearsal to the next.

In doing this it is important to remember that the amount of rehearsal time afforded by any given production period can vary enormously: you may have plenty of time to enjoy the process or you may have very little. While it would be hoped that you will experience long and luxuriant rehearsal schedules during your time as a theatre practitioner, it is reasonable to expect that shorter and sharper ones will probably be more common; in some cases, your amount of rehearsal time is likely to be very short indeed. For this reason, it is vital that your methodology when working practically upon character is robust and capable enough to be effective in haste as well as at leisure. Although the process in shorter time frames

Pure and truthful characterization.

may not be as fully rounded and extensive as when afforded the luxury of longer ones, it must still be able to complete the job as effectively as possible. An audience will not appreciate, or even be aware of, the time taken to realize the production they are watching, but will still be judgmental, albeit subconsciously, in regard to your ability to convince them of reality, spontaneity, naturalness and truth.

You should also be mindful of the fact that all of your practical application of research and analysis upon character must be processed, accessed and interpreted through you as an individual. You cannot create characters out of thin air or construct them from scratch. They must live through you as a real and living person in your own right – indeed, this is the most unique and positive feature of dramatic art. Therefore, your research and analysis of character must always be mindful of this and you should never forget that a very important part of your primary source material is yourself. Do not try to impose a character upon your own personality but find it through, and in harmony with, what you already have and who you already are. You are 'real' and your characters must be 'real' also because of this and not despite it.

The Importance of 'Feel'

During normal everyday life a person is not generally aware of the elements that combine to communicate their personalities to the outside world. As you go about your daily life you do not, in general, have a constant awareness of how you are moving, talking, walking and appearing to others. In fact, if you did, life would become intolerably inhibiting. However, you are 'aware' of yourself; you 'feel' like you and this feeling is constantly manifest and affects the way you proceed and function. This feeling is obviously very much centred upon your own perception of how you

appear to others and the world and may not be fully in accord with a more objective outside viewpoint, but it is, nonetheless, wholly and exclusively your 'feel', the thing that keeps you in daily touch with yourself and your individual soul.

In the same way it is the 'feel' of a character that you must ultimately find and, more importantly, be at total ease with. It is the aim of all character research and analysis to develop living beings from printed words and, in order to do this successfully, not only must the characteristics that you find work seamlessly together to create a natural embodiment of fiction, but they must grow and develop organically throughout the process of creation so that, rather than manufacturing characters with countable particular details, you give birth to characters with a myriad of uncountable, interlinked and ever increasing traits that work in perfect and automatic harmony to communicate a truthful depiction of a human being in all its complexity.

It is the 'feel' of a character (correctly achieved and realized) that will enable you to develop this fictitious person, adding gradually but realistically to their persona and constantly finding new but truthful insights into portraying them effectively. Although you may start with bold and practical decisions as to their way of moving and sounding, this must mutate from an 'outside' perception of detail to an 'inside' understanding of their 'feel'.

Although you may find this difficult to understand at first, as you work through your practical application to character building you will begin to find yourself appreciating the benefits of feeling what your character is really like, rather than just knowing how they look and sound. The ultimate aim here is to replicate real life in the sense that a person is aware of himself or herself internally rather than externally. When you finally take your character in front of an expectant audience you should be no more cognizant of their detailed appearance than you are of your own. However, you should be very aware of, and responsive to, their 'feel'.

A character must 'feel' right.

A STARTING PLACE

If you have followed the advice of this book so far you will, hypothetically, approach every first rehearsal already armed with considerable research regarding your character's background, personality and place within the

scheme of the play. All of this will have been sourced from the text of the work, historical and geographical fact and your own imagination and creativity, all in measures appropriate to the particular play you are working on. You will also have, at the very least, started the process of analysis, in as much as you will have begun to find for yourself the significance of these facts in terms of the artistic intentions of the play and your character's role within its plot, purpose and theme.

Now comes the time when all of this work must justify itself when it is put into practice. Fortunately, acting is not essentially about knowledge (knowledge has a huge part to play but, totally in terms of furthering the acting, it is not an end in itself) but about *doing* and *being* – it is very much a participation activity. What is very much needed then at this stage is a way of translating all of the research and analysis (thus far, purely cerebral) into the beginnings of a practical creation. This is not a new part of the process but merely a continuation of it, but now conducted in different, more immediate terms. However, this translation can be difficult and hard-earned research may be wasted if things go wrong at this juncture, so the commencement of rehearsal must be handled carefully.

Poised with an armoury of research at your fingertips, you may need a way of kick-starting all of this into the beginnings of characterization. It might well be helpful to look at the rehearsal process stage by stage – not in literal terms, and this will vary depending upon the production and the director, but in terms of how you approach each practical development on the route from page to stage as it were.

Stage One

There will come a time when your private work alone with the script, and your various sources of research, will be ended and you must venture forth and speak the lines for the first time. This may be during an initial read-through with the cast, the 'blocking' of the play (the early determination of the moves) or the first working of the play, as some directors prefer to work as they block rather than blocking quickly first. However it manifests itself, this is the first moment (amongst many to come) of truth.

For all talk of 'feel', this will rarely emerge this early and your first inevitable considerations will be how the character should walk and talk. This in itself will be no problem as the results of your research will be more than ready to inform this. However, knowing what to do and actually doing it effectively can be two very different things, and this is as true in acting as it is in life generally. In order to make the jump into a practical application of your study it is often useful (or perhaps necessary) to have a particular image, 'hook' or 'handle' to get things started.

To fully understand the need for this, a useful and illuminating analogy may be drawn from the sport of golf. A golf swing is an immensely complicated action, with many component parts, all of which must function properly for the whole action to be successful. It is almost impossible to focus upon each of these components individually at the time of making the swing, so a golfer will often rely upon a simple visualization of what is happening as a whole in order to allow his or her body and mind to flow freely and thus automatically execute each detail correctly.

Likewise, an actor may find it just as difficult to execute the complex subtleties of movement and sound in the early stages of rehearsal, however clearly and knowledgeably they may understand them in theory. A golfer may also have a particular mental image in order to start the swing smoothly and so too may the actor in order to start the process of moving from research to characterization in practice.

107

For the actor, this initiatory device should be something that can be identified as a particularly prevalent characteristic or personality trait exhibited by the character being played. For instance, a predisposition towards an attitude of cynicism may just be enough to give the character its first 'voice', or a deep-seated anger may provide an emotional key to unlocking a character initially.

It is worth recognizing at this point that a character within a play (as with a person in real life) will emit a character trait either generally within their personality or in particular when placed in certain circumstances. The hero of a tragedy may have an ingrained cynicism resulting from their bitter and dramatic experience of life, while a detective in a thriller may take a cynical approach to interrogating a particular suspect. Likewise the former may have been made irrevocably and characteristically angry by their exposure to suffering, while the detective may be angry at being told lies by the villain of the piece.

Either of these scenarios will prove adequate for the purpose of a starting point – all you should be looking for here is a 'way in'. What is of vital importance is that you do not become stuck with a particular attitude and thus inhibit the development of the character generally. There will be many aspects to the character that, having identified them from hard study, you will want to portray. You may use one of these to create a mental image as a tool of instigation but, having done this, do not let it blind you to the fullness of characterization that you ultimately seek. To use the golf analogy once more, you must always remember to 'follow through' with your characterization.

Stage Two

You will now be past the formative stages of rehearsal and getting into your stride. If all is working well you will be finding out fast how your character presents themselves to the world; you will be gaining confidence in their movement, speech, posture and mannerisms; you will be discovering their attitudes to the other characters in the play and their place within the universe it creates. Importantly, in addition, you will also be finding out which pieces of your research and analysis work best, which are perhaps suspect in their usefulness and which need to be further studied and developed.

It will be useful to keep in mind the following checklist of important points as you navigate this critical stage of character development.

- You must find the character within yourself. No amount of research and understanding of the person you are playing will negate the fact that they have to achieve life via your body, voice and soul.
- Keep open-minded about all of the character's personality traits and do not focus upon any one exclusively, even if you have used this to initially start the process.
- Remember that acting is a group activity. Listen hard to the other actors as they speak their lines and watch them carefully. Consider their reactions to your character as an invaluable part of your research.
- Relish the opportunity of finding the physicality of the character. Do not force this process but let it come naturally and organically from your research and acquired understanding.
- Do not try to identify and control every aspect of the character's being. Let them start to live automatically and begin to take you over.
- Relaxed concentration in rehearsals is far better than frantic tension. Have faith in yourself as an actor and your character as a living being.

A consideration of all these points will begin to lead you towards the illusive 'feel'.

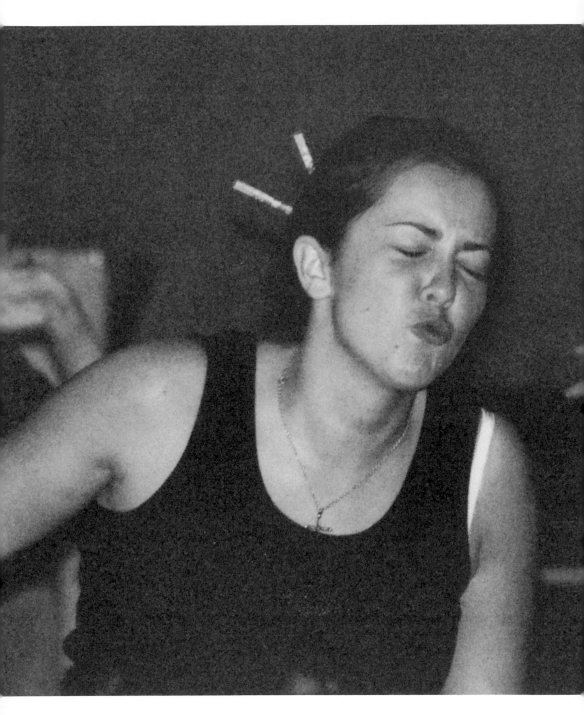

A characterization begins to work.

Stage Three

As 'feel' now begins to develop, your characterization should really take off. Feeling how your character is, rather than just knowing, is extremely invigorating and conformational in telling you that you have got the process right. It is also wonderfully liberating as you find yourself developing the character almost without being aware that you are doing so. One aspect of characterization will seamlessly, effortlessly and automatically lead to another and each individual detail, being based primarily upon your 'feel' for the character rather than cerebral decision-making, will be pertinent and truthful to the whole.

At this stage you should not perceive any real difference between yourself and the character. This is not to say that the character has become the same as you in terms of personality or vice versa, but that your portrayal of the character should feel as instinctive and holistic to you as your own self, perhaps, ironically, more so.

It is only by feeling your characters in this way that you will present them truthfully. It is impossible to be truthful if you are continuously attempting to talk, walk, gesture and so on in certain ways and by conscious means. While this may be necessary at Stage One and acceptable at Stage Two, it is most definitely a sign of failure by Stage Three. Stage Three must be all about instinct, subconscious subtlety, implicit complexity and automatic adherence to truth via a spontaneous and self-perpetuating reality of characterization. Although this is obviously very much an ideal, it is an ideal to which all of your research and analysis will comfortably lead you if done properly and diligently.

Stage Four

You will by now have a total belief in your character. This is vital – before an audience can believe in an actor's creation the actor must

An Actor's Diary

The following is a fictitious diary extract from the first five days of a play rehearsal period. Although somewhat idealized it will help to illuminate a strong and positive mental attitude as the work progresses.

Day One: Arrived at rehearsals. My mind is chock-full of my study of the play so far and what I hope to achieve with my characterization. It's a relief to meet the others and not to be working on my own any more. The read-through was great fun and I was able to experiment with some of my ideas. Gained inspiration from what some of the others were doing too. All looks promising.

Day Two: Completed the 'blocking' today'. Much easier to get an overall impression of what I am aiming for now. Started detailed work on the first act. Received some very positive input from the director. We seem to be on the same wavelength.

Day Three: The character is working well. Playing him/her with so much anger initially really seems to have got me off to a good start. Now beginning to mellow the character a little and explore other avenues of personality.

Day Four: Am now really starting to get a 'feel' for the character. My voice sounds right and my movements are becoming instinctive. All of the background research I have done on the play and the character is really paying dividends now.

Day Five: Really started to interact well with the other characters today. Some of the scenes are working very well indeed. The director seems pleased and I think this is going to be a good production.

believe in it themselves. Having obtained this belief you have reached your goal of bringing a fictitious character to life. This is not to say that

An actor relaxes during rehearsals.

the process is complete; a properly constructed performance will continue to develop and grow over the entire life of a production and the work will never be entirely finished until the final curtain. Indeed, even then, an actor may hope to play the part again and explore the character still further.

Understanding by Example

Having briefly reviewed this practical process of character building and obtained an overview, it will now be useful for you to practise this in order to begin to broaden understanding and move towards creating a methodology that will work for you in particular. It will be best to do this in as simple and focused way as possible. The following extract from Shakespeare's *Much Ado About Nothing* will introduce you to two of the Bard's most fascinating and complex characters. Read the play, work upon the characters in all the ways suggested and then practise and develop your 'feel' as you learn and perform the text, preferably with a willing partner. Remember to use this exercise as fully as possible and indulge yourself with copious research and analysis.

BEATRICE
Will you not tell me who told you so?

BENEDICK
No, you shall pardon me.

BEATRICE
Nor will you not tell me who you are?

BENEDICK
Not now.

BEATRICE
That I was disdainful, and that I had my good wit out of the 'Hundred Merry Tales:' — well this was Signior Benedick that said so.

BENEDICK
What's he?

BEATRICE
I am sure you know him well enough.

BENEDICK
Not I, believe me.

BEATRICE
Did he never make you laugh?

BENEDICK
I pray you, what is he?

BEATRICE
Why, he is the prince's jester: a very dull fool; only his gift is in devising impossible slanders: none but libertines delight in him; and the commendation is not in his wit, but in his villany; for he both pleases men and angers them, and then they laugh at him and beat him. I am sure he is in the fleet: I would he had boarded me.

BENEDICK
When I know the gentleman, I'll tell him what you say.

BEATRICE
Do, do: he'll but break a comparison or two on me; which, peradventure not marked or not laughed at, strikes him into melancholy; and then there's a partridge wing saved, for the fool will eat no supper that night.

Music

We must follow the leaders.

BENEDICK
In every good thing.

BEATRICE
Nay, if they lead to any ill, I will leave them at the next turning.

Dance. Then exeunt.

9   PUTTING IT ALL TOGETHER

THE CONTRIBUTORS

This book has so far concentrated upon actors and directors in reference to its examination of understanding text. This chapter will continue to do so but, as its modus operandi is to take an overview of the whole production process in relation to the overall interpretation of a script, it will also investigate the roles of other possible members of the production team.

It is quite likely that you may find yourself performing one of these other tasks at some time, either as part of your other responsibilities or in a more dedicated fashion. Even if this is not so, an understanding of all the elements of the undertakings, and their relationship to the play that is being worked upon, will be invaluable in strengthening your abilities generally.

There are many people involved with a production.

The Director

It is the director who is usually the only person within the company who will start work upon the production completely from scratch. At this point there is only a script, a play full of words and stage directions – a blank canvas upon which the director must begin to formulate an interpretation. Of course, it is very possible that this play will come with some 'baggage': it will have a reputation; there will have been past productions that the director may have seen or known about; there may be controversy linked to it in some way – all factors that might possibly threaten to have some influence. However, provided the director has an open-minded and relaxed attitude to the play's past, it should represent reasonably pliant and malleable material, clean and fresh for the production to come. It is equally possible too, that this will be the very first production of the play, in which case it will constitute an amazingly exciting prospect.

There are four possible scenarios connected to the director's initial relationship with the play:

1. They may have been given the play to direct and may have no previous knowledge of it.
2. They may have been given the play to direct but do have previous knowledge of it, to whatever degree.
3. They may have chosen the play to direct and therefore not only have previous knowledge of it but have some kind of emotional or intellectual attachment to it.
4. They may have written the play themselves, in which case the emotional and intellectual attachment will be very strong indeed.

Each of these possibilities will require the director to structure their early work, order their priorities and observe their responsibilities in slightly different ways. There follow some important pointers for a director's starting strategy for each of the possibilities in turn.

1. This is no bad situation. To have no previous knowledge of the text, while potentially more arduous a prospect, is also to have no prejudices or entrenched view about it, and so negates the necessity to deal with these. However, it places a greater responsibility upon the director to become cognizant with all of the play's attributes, possible failings and possible potentials from cold. The play should be read through several times and the initial response to it should be allowed to form naturally and gradually. Not taking enough time at this early stage could be disastrous. As with all drama, solid foundations are essential for the 'building' to come.
2. It is very easy in this case to become lazy and not do enough preparatory work. Nothing should be assumed about the play and it must be reread carefully to enable it to expose itself afresh to the director. It is very often surprising just how much can be missed, falsely remembered and misinterpreted from a play that is seemingly familiar. The director should not take anything for granted and, while not ignoring previous reactions to the play, new ones should be allowed to form.
3. There is even more risk of a closed mind here. It is certainly wonderful for a director to work upon a play that they love and respect, and the energetic sense of purpose that the opportunity to make their mark upon it that this will engender is marvellous for any production. However, the pitfalls just need to be observed and avoided: the more of an 'attitude' a director has towards a text, the more likely they are to miss something important or ignore a broader view. Provided they remind themselves of this and remain detached, to a certain extent,

there will be no problem at all and they are very likely to create a definitive production.

4. There are obvious advantages in a director directing their own play, in as much as nobody can possibly know or understand the work better. However, there are also considerable dangers, mainly being that of a massive magnification of those risks mentioned in point three: a director will be very, and quite naturally, predisposed to a closed mind regarding interpretation. There is also another negative factor to consider: in such circumstances the unique 'three-way' partnership between author, practitioner and audience (talked of earlier in the book) is totally corrupted and lost. The very special artistic process, as a director takes the play from the playwright and respectfully builds upon it with interpretation, is completely non-existent and the dramatic form reverts back towards the two-way process of other art forms. Although it may be necessary, even wise overall, for the writer to direct the work, this should not be undertaken without careful thought and, at the very least, the consideration of whether a separate director might be employed if financially possible.

It having been established that the director is now fully familiar with the play, and mindful of all the possible drawbacks of any previous relationship with it, the process of interpretation must begin. As previously mentioned, this process is usually initiated by the director and this is an onerous task indeed.

The first responsibility of the director is to formulate the main thrust, angle or direction that the interpretation is to take. All drama needs to be researched, analysed and interpreted – this is what makes it unique and is the very reason for your reading of this book – but it is the director's overall, encompassing and enlightening concept for a production that provides a 'peg' on which all the other members of the team may 'hang' their own contributions.

It is important that this 'concept' of the director does not become a gimmick or allow itself to be perceived as a corruption or distortion of the play's material. It is often said that a play has been 'mucked about with' and, while this is sometimes an unfair and ill-informed reaction to genuine interpretation, it is also often true. The most often heard example of this criticism is when it is directed at a production of Shakespeare that is accused of being in 'modern dress' or of not being done 'like it was in the olden days'. While it is very easy to view such comments as ignorant, and to remind such detractors that Shakespeare's original productions were all in 'modern dress' and interpreted in their own way, it should also be noted that such criticisms are often the result of dishonest, unsubstantiated interpretations and therefore partially valid however poorly expressed.

There can be no doubt that inventive, considered and inspirational interpretation of a play is essential to a great production, but it must always be based upon an honest analysis of the text and soundly rooted in a truthful observation of the play's intentions. An interpretation should not try to be 'clever' or impose itself upon the play. Rather, it should work in harmony with the text, enabling and empowering it without patronizing it or taking it for granted.

As it is the director who instigates the process of interpretation, so it is the director who is responsible for making sure that it is interpretation with a purpose and not manipulation for its own sake. As an example, and to use Shakespeare for it once again, if a director were, say, to be heading up a production of *Macbeth* and deciding to set it in the environment of a large, modern corporate company, with the eponymous *Macbeth* as a would-be managing director, then she or he would need

to be sure that such a concept was based upon an informed and considered personal understanding of the play's themes rather than a cheap and easy way of costuming.

In the context of this example, it is impossible to decide if this particular concept is good or bad: for it is not the concept itself that is of importance in this regard but how the director justifies it and then executes it in accordance with that justification. Everything that a director does within a production must have substance and must be firmly based upon an honest and truthful reaction to the text. In these terms, one director may make a huge success of a most outlandish and flamboyant rendition of a well-known play, while another may flounder and fail with a more modest but less personally inspired one.

Concepts must be strong but truthful.

So then, the director's early musing upon the play must be geared towards discovering what the text says and means to them and formulating an idea and perception of how these insights may be used to bring life to a script in production. The initial concept may be large or small; it may be full and detailed, such as a particular period or situation within which to set the play, or it may be of less substance but of equal interpretational intent, such as a determination to gently highlight one particular aspect or theme of the play. However, most importantly, it must have integrity – it must be born of the director's well-meaning desire to allow the text to 'speak' with as clear and uninhibited a 'voice' as possible and not simply of a wish to be applauded and garlanded for the ingenuity of the concept itself.

It is reasonably true that some plays are more suited to specific interpretation than others. For instance, Shakespeare's plays are generally open to decisions of setting, period and style while the work of, for example, J.B. Priestley is basically narrow and predetermined in these matters. However, there is often some possibility for interpretational manoeuvring in the unlikeliest of works; a shallow, badly written thriller, with two-dimensional characters and an unbelievable plot, may be given some semblance of substantiality by the director deciding that it should be played pantomimically, thus making a feature of the banality and finding a curious way of making it work within the production.

Of course, no decision should be reached by any director regarding the nature of any particular concept or blueprint for interpretation, without first ensuring that a full, preliminary research of the play has been undertaken. This book is full of information regarding why, how and when this should be done, but it is worth emphasizing here that the effort involved in such an enterprise finds its first rewards in the formulation of a good, solid and substantial concept or idea for the production. The more initial study that is done and the deeper the director has looked into the factual detail of the play, in all of its manifestations, then the more likely the concept, thus derived, is to succeed, and the less likely it is to be suspect in its integrity, truth and honesty.

Having found the basic concept for the production, and having made sure of its justification, the director must then enter the rehearsal period with the task of enabling the actors to do their jobs of playing the various characters within the story. These actors must be gently and respectfully led into an understanding and appreciation of the director's ideas, but must

also be encouraged, helped and empowered to bring their own ideas and philosophies about the play into the equation. This relationship between director and actor has already been examined and requires no more illumination here, except to reiterate that the director has a primary responsibility to ensure that an actor has an understanding of the material, is in tune with the concept and has confidence in the performance, for it is the actor who must step upon the stage and 'take the flack', not the director.

The Designer

One of the first appointments that a director is likely to make (or have made for them by the production manager), when embarking upon a new production, is a meeting with the designer for a preliminary but vitally important discussion about the set and 'look' generally. This may take place on a one-to-one basis or as part of a full-blown initial production meeting, although, in such cases, it is likely that some amount of 'chat' will have already passed between the two, perhaps on the telephone. This is a crucial encounter, for the designer's input into the overall thematic scheme of the production, particularly at this early stage, is vital to the eventual outcome.

It is on this occasion that the director will semi-formally present his or her ideas and the designer has the opportunity of asking questions and generally making sure they clearly understand the concept as presented. Although the designer will not be expected to create a 'design' for the show on the spot, they are very likely to express their initial thoughts as to how the production may be achieved and engage in a free flow of further ideas and inspirations with the director and other members of the production crew, if they are present. The very best of these meetings tend to become a kind of 'brainstorming' session, with uninhibited discussion aimed at uncovering and airing various possibilities, many of which will not be brought to fruition (or even seriously considered) but others sticking and developing into key production elements. Some decisions may need to be made at this stage but only those that are really necessary prior to the presentation of the design at a later date.

One important factor that will be discussed and finalized will be the budget, for the resources available will be crucial to the way in which all ideas by all contributors will finally be achieved.

Having ascertained what the director requires, and having made complementary contributions to the now fully emerging concept, it becomes the designer's task to pull this together into a practical and creatable blueprint for how the production will look and work in practice. This may be just in terms of the set or include the costumes too (although there

may well be a separate costume designer if budget allows). This work will be in anticipation of another meeting when the 'design' will be presented, very often in the form of a model box containing the proposed set to scale.

It is now that the designer will become very much engaged in their own research. The research undertaken by the designer is of particular interest because, although they will be investigating within the same areas and using the same methods as theatrical research generally, the fruits of their particular labours have a very real and concrete significance. This is because the factual knowledge they acquire will be directly translated into a physical reality. It may be pertinent for a director to understand the type of house a particular character

A stage set must be well designed.

from a particular period play would reside in, but the precision of this knowledge is not of dire consequence. However, a designer's understanding of this information is specifically crucial, as they must actually put the results of their research into action and re-create the said environment in a way that will be directly accountable to an audience and sharp-eyed critics.

There can be no more practical and crucial application of research than this: a designer is researching, not just in terms of artistic integrity, but also of precise and defendable practicality; the 'look' must look right; the detail must be correct. Obviously, the more specific the period and social requirements of the piece the greater the factual accuracy must be. Some productions may lend themselves to a more general and metaphoric simulation of reality, but, to a major degree, a designer's researching process must be real, immediate, unambiguous and direct.

In the same way, so must the designer's analysis, based upon their compiled research, be fool-proofed against critical scrutiny. Any decisions a director makes, based upon the evidence of their research, may be viewed as personally interpretational and given the benefit of the doubt, and within the metaphorical layering of the presentation of performances may not be accountably identifiable anyway. However, decisions made by the designer, informed by much the same quality of research, will be immortalized within a tangible, physical and ultimately evidential setting; a designer is far more of a 'sitting target'.

The Stage Management

While the research of all other members of the production team contain at least some degree of artistic elitism, the production manager has a most down-to-earth and workaday reason for research and equally unromantic results. In saying 'Production Manager' here, it should be

The 'Design' Discipline

There is a strong lesson to be learned from the accuracy of research that is required by a designer, encompassing two points:

1. If ever you become involved in the process of design (either formally as a designer as such or in terms of contributing to a design process) be very sure that your research is accurate, that you understand fully the results of it, and that the analytical and interpretational decisions you make upon it are sound, defendable and honest in integrity; the evidence upon which you will be judged is recordable.
2. As humble director or actor, assume that the disciplined accuracy necessary of a designer's study is your guide. Do not be sloppy in your research just because it may be easier for you to get away with it; do not be shallow or dishonest in your analysis just because the overall result may be acceptable; and always make all of your work accountable to scrutiny, however and wherever that scrutiny may or may not come from.

made clear that the actual personnel or job title involved in this type of task may vary depending upon the production and its resources. There may not be a Production Manger but only a Stage Manager and, if there is a Production Manager, he or she (for many of the best stage management personnel are women) may well be too busy to be involved in the type of research referred to here and may delegate this anyway. However, whoever is responsible for leaving the production meeting with the stage managerial application of the decided overall concept of production as their responsibility, will be faced with the most mundane, practical, thankless and essentially vital and indispensable research task of all.

Props are an important part of stage management.

Whoever is in charge, there will hopefully be a stage management team, all of whom will be responsible for various aspects of the production process, which vary according to the particular stage management 'set-up' or organization of personnel. (This team may also be responsible for constructing, or at least assembling the set, or this may be sourced from outside the company.) For the sake of clarity, and because different jobs may be done by different people in different companies, it will be helpful to refer to the team collectively as 'stage management' and to have an approximate overview of all of the responsibilities that they are likely to have.

Much of the stage management's research will be concerned with the arduous task of discovering the best and cheapest way of making the artistic inspirations of the director and designer work in practice. There will inevitably be a necessary preoccupation with the minutiae of construction: obtaining and using the right kind of screws, hinges, brackets and handles; whether or not the stage floor can be painted; finding suitable transportation; identifying access and working restrictions in the theatre; checking that the dimensions upon the ground plan match the actual stage.

It must be remembered that much of the work involved with staging a production is something of a building project, but it is one with a difference: the build must be quick, economic, non-permanent, practical to the demands of a fictitious story, actor proof, and be located in an area designed for audience viewing (often in one direction) and with a stage that very usually slopes from back to front (the 'rake'). The achievement of all this requires ingenuity and an ability to source materials quickly, cheaply and effectively. In its own way, finding a method of making a theatre production work, with all of the associated guile, cunning and resourcefulness that is needed, is a research project of great magnitude.

While the venues of research for actors and directors may be libraries and museums, the hunting grounds for stage management are more likely to be hardware stores and builder's yards. The most useful method of researching that a stage management team member can employ is finding, meeting and cultivating the acquaintance of those likely to be helpful and obliging in terms of providing materials and services cheaply or (better still) for free. Good stage management will always possess an ever-growing list of 'mates' upon whom they can call to solve the most difficult of problems.

However, not all stage management research is concerned with the 'nuts and bolts' of production. One of their more interesting jobs (although no less demanding) is the obtaining of props and appropriate fittings for the stage. Very often there will be a varied array of crockery, cutlery, pottery, ornamentation, light shades, door handles and general clutter to collect. These may be purchased, borrowed and, very often, begged from around the town in which the production is to have its home.

Again, if it is a period piece then a good degree of accuracy will be needed in sourcing the right objects in a suitable condition, and this can be just as difficult when working upon a more recent period of history as it will for a distant one. The designer may pass on a good deal of research regarding the type of material props needed but, if not, the stage management must do their homework to ensure that they are sourcing the correct stock. Indeed, it is as well for them to check the details of what they are to acquire anyway for, when things go wrong, it is usually the stage management who get the blame and certainly who will have to put it right. When working on historical plays, the cultivation of a friendly antique shopowner can be hugely advantageous.

Actors Should Stage Manage

It is vitally important that actors and directors understand the work of stage management. Their work is absolutely essential to the overall results of the production process and, without them, all of the brilliant artistic insights explored and the development in rehearsal would come to nothing. Actors and directors can very easily be insensitive towards stage management and fail to appreciate just what an important and sustaining role they play; in some cases they can feel totally taken for granted and unappreciated.

This is not just a question of team dynamics and empathizing with your colleagues; understanding the process of stage management will be invaluable in helping you to become a better theatre practitioner generally. There is absolutely no doubt that some of the best actors and directors are those who have done stage management themselves. Therefore, the very best way for you to gain a knowledge of the stage management process is to become involved and do some. Knowing how a production physically and practically makes it onto the stage will be invaluable in aiding you to become better at your research, interpretation and every other aspect of your vocation.

As well as their fair share of research, the stage management are not without the need for analysis either. However, there is again a very different emphasis. While the director and actors are busy in rehearsals analysing, say, the relationship between the characters and their environment, the stage management may be just as fervently analysing how to stop a door swinging open against the steep rake of the stage. While this is obviously a slightly facetious example, it serves as a very important lesson: work upon drama is not essentially about pretension or academic indulgence; the concerns of all your actions will be totally directed towards the very practical task of entertaining, informing and emotionally affecting your audience and, in achieving this, finding out how to make a door stay closed is just as important as understanding how slums of Victorian London affected the lives of its citizens.

The Lighting Designer

For those audience members who are not actively involved in the production of drama themselves, the lighting of a play is something they very often take totally for granted. They certainly appreciate it (and the vital contribution it makes to their enjoyment of the show) but this usually registers subconsciously and becomes an unidentifiable element of their overall critique. Although this is probably as it should be in many ways, it is a shame that the effectiveness of good lighting is not more obvious to the uninitiated.

The contribution made by a good lighting designer to the production as a whole is enormous. Without lights the most elaborate of sets will look lifeless and incredibly talented actors will not be seen. However, lighting is not just a case of illumination but of the skilful enhancement of atmosphere and environment. A poorly lit production can be ruined but a well-lit one can be enhanced beyond measure.

Once again, the lighting designer may hold a dedicated post within the team or, when necessary, may double up as the production or stage manager. Whatever the case, it is a job the importance of which should not be underestimated.

There is a rather interesting and unique aspect to the type of research and analysis required of the lighting designer, for it is actually the work of the other team members that must be studied in order to perfect a lighting design. Although there will be collaboration and discussion with the director and the designer from the start (with an important role to play in the initial production meeting as well), the lighting designer will not formalize or finalize his or her design until they have watched some of the rehearsals and probably not until late in the rehearsal period, perhaps at a final run-through.

In this way, they will study what the actors and directors have done with the piece, they will absorb the atmosphere that they have created, they will determine a feel for the dynamics of the production and they will acquire knowledge of significant moments in the overall flow of the plot. They will also ascertain the main areas of the stage that are being used and their importance and relevance to the action. It is only then that they will be able to integrate these findings with their own ideas about the production and make concrete decisions about the lights and their usage.

Thus the work of others becomes part of a lighting designer's research topic and criteria. There can be no better example of how 'understanding text' is very much a communal process.

The Sound Designer

There is even less likelihood that there will be a dedicated sound designer in the team (although a great asset if there is), the job usually being the responsibility of stage management or, more probably, the Theatre's sound technician or operator. Again this is a very important task, as sound can make or break a production.

In many ways the role of the sound design will follow the same pattern as the lighting in terms of its execution. However, there is an additional responsibility by way of accuracy. For example, if a director asks for a sound cue containing birdsong, the sound designer cannot simply produce the first bit of recorded birdsong they find, as it may be a totally inappropriate sound. They must ascertain the nature of the fictitious location in which the sound is supposedly heard, the time of day, the types of birds likely to be singing and degree and frequency of their audibility. The same research must be taken for most other sounds: the type of train, the volume of traffic, the intensity of the storm, the density of the crowd,

Good sound can make a production.

and so on. It will not be necessary to directly concern themselves with the volume of sound at this stage, as this will be decided upon and 'set' by the director during the technical rehearsal. However, it may be useful for them to have a good working knowledge of the auditorium acoustically so that they can guide the director towards appropriate sound levels and predict any likely adjustments to be made when an audience is in the 'house', soaking up the sound.

The sound designer will have three main sources of research in determining the nature and quality of the sound plot: the script, watching rehearsals and, most vitally, the director, who will have a good idea of what they want but may welcome the sound designer's expert help and advice in determining the exact nature of the sound effects for any given scene.

Another part of the sound designer's expertise lies in a knowledge and ability to source the correct sounds and to record them for the

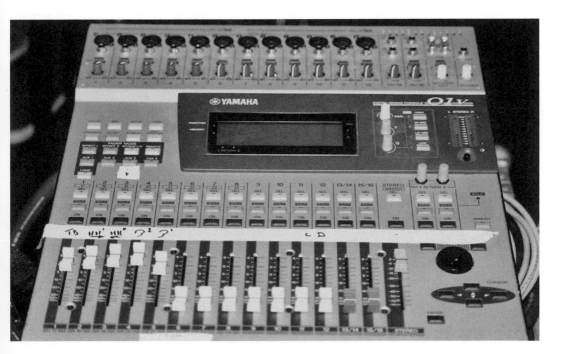

production clearly and accurately. Sound effects can be found on dedicated CDs and tapes, old vinyl records and archival recording of other productions. However, by far the best and most accessible source now is the Internet, where it is possible to find practically any kind of sound effect to download at a certain cost or even for free. It is a very good idea for anyone involved in theatrical sound to spend some time trawling the web for suitable material and building up a personal library for use later.

Having obtained the sounds, they must be recorded onto the show tape (or, more probably, digital device) with care. The sound designer must make sure that the sounds are pure with as little extraneous noise as possible, and that they are edited tightly so that they will play immediately upon cue.

The Wardrobe Department

As already mentioned, there may or may not be a costume designer on the production team. If not, the task of costume design will fall within the remit and research criteria of the production designer. However, it is likely that the day-to-day practicalities of the costumes will revert to the costume department, be this a wardrobe mistress or a co-opted section of the stage management. Apart from the similar considerations regarding period accuracy required for the set (and the furniture in front of it for that matter) in terms of the actual garments, care, consideration and research needs to be taken with the actual wearing of the costumes and, in particular, the partnering and use of accessories.

A good wardrobe department will make sure that all details, however extraneous, are correct, and should also help and advise the actors as to suitable methods of movement, posture and general style when dressed in them as character. This attention to detail will provide an interesting opportunity for research and cumulative acquisition of useful background knowledge. It is also an area that links very firmly to a particular character and also all members of the production team (especially the director and actors) who should become involved in the decision-making connected with the selection and wearing of costume. For instance, would a *certain* character in a *certain* situation wear a *certain* item of clothing or carry a *certain* accessory, even if the style of their social position and class might suggest it? Is this character a conformist – conventional and fashionable in dress according to the time, or a maverick – a convention breaker with their very own sense of style and application of the contemporary trends.

It is interesting when considering this example to see just how interlinked the various aspects of production are in terms of studying text. No actor's performance, however researched, analysed, interpreted and technically perfected it may be, can exist properly in a vacuum or, at least, not owe their existence, in part, to several other members of the team. A decision about movement can be informed, guided, even decided upon by the provision, from wardrobe, of a particular pair of shoes – thus the selection of shoes becomes part of the rehearsal process and the rehearsal process part of the selection of the shoes; a particularly refined method of holding a teacup, painstakingly researched in social and historical detail, will actually be made possible by the selection of just the right tea service of impeccable delicacy, and impossible by just the wrong one of clumsy chunkiness; a suggested choice of style or colour can provide the inspiration to tie various stands of research and study into a workable performance.

The Publicity Department

Although publicity is not usually directly part of the production team, it is very much a contributory factor in the success (or otherwise) of a production and, therefore, its relationship to researching drama is worth considering.

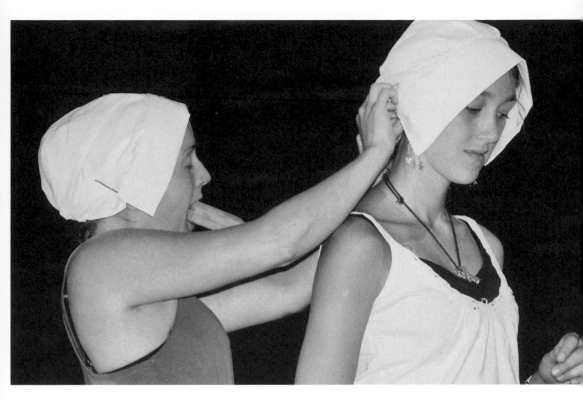

Appropriate costume is also vital.

Of all the various departments involved in bringing a play to life it is the one that is most often criticized by the others (sometimes justifiably so), and this is probably because of the difficulty involved in doing the job properly and the destructive potential upon any venture if it is not. Good publicity, properly targeted, is invaluable but poor publicity, carelessly directed, can be a waste of resources and a liability. Once again, the main preparatory activity for successful marketing is the subject of this book: that is, research and analysis. A good publicity manager will research and analyse in two major ways:

1. They will research the play, find out what it is about, how it is to be produced, who is to be in it, and so on, and then analyse the best way to market it.
2. They will research the potential audience for such a play within the given location of

the Theatre, and then analyse the best way of reaching them and grabbing their attention.

It is not necessary to examine the various methods that may be employed for successful publicity here, but it is worth encouraging you, as a theatre practitioner, to help and become involved with the process. If a publicity department is not using you as a means for their research, that is, they are not asking you about the play and how it is taking shape in rehearsals, then give them the information anyway. A publicity manager is not at all rehearsals (although, in an ideal world, they should be invited to, and attend, at least one or two) and therefore they do not have immediate recourse to the very information they need to sell the play. You are an ideal source of compensation for this and you should not only volunteer your help but encourage them to use you as much as possible. Suggest to them that you attend interviews with the local media and make sure that they are kept up to date with each new development of the production: good publicity is the responsibility of all, as without it, all other effort is negated.

Here again is an example of how a theatre practitioner is not only a researcher and analyser but a source of research and analysis, too. If you were ever in doubt that drama and the studying of text with a view to performance is a wholly communal activity, then you should certainly not be by now.

Everyone can get involved in promoting a show.

Marketing Responsibility

There is also a particular way in which your personal study may link very successfully with the efforts of the publicity department. During your research you may well discover an important fact, connected to the historical or social viewpoint of the play, that proves to be an ideal marketing focus point, either in terms of an interesting 'angle' to promote the material (an unusual factor that will arouse interest and perhaps even controversy), or of direct relevance to the potential audience (a local historical figure connected to the story or an element of the theme with a particular significance for a local group or faction). In such a case, the sharing of this will mean both you and the production generally will greatly benefit from your labours.

10 A PLAY TO PRACTISE ON

Use this example of a full-length play to practise all of your skills of research, analysis and interpretation. As an exercise, try to utilize every possible facet of these disciplines. Return to each chapter of the book in turn and apply it to this text in as many ways as you possibly can. Its potential for part historical, part mythological research, coupled with its colourful characters, should keep you busy for quite a while. You will also find opportunities to consider set, lighting, sound and stage management.

The cast loosen up.

KING ARTHUR'S QUEST
BY JOHN HESTER

Merlin
Sir Lancelot

Apprentice 1
Boy Arthur
Morgan Le Fay

Apprentice 2
King Uther
King Arthur
Invisible Knight
Black Knight

Apprentice 3
Sir Kay
Lady of the Lake
Queen Guinevere

Apprentice 4
Sir Ector
Sir Galahad
Sir Mordred

No unauthorized performance of this play.

Pre-show: Sir Galahad, buffoonish and quite out of character with his name, meets and greets the audience, chats to them, samples their sweets and so on. He may be accompanied by other characters.

1. MERLIN'S CAVERN

Merlin and his four apprentices (hooded)

> MERLIN
> Loyal and faithful apprentices — students in the ancient art of magic and enchantment, do you hear me?

> APPRENTICE 1
> We are present, Merlin — oh great Master Magician, and await your command.

> MERLIN
> To us has been given a duty most onerous. We, practitioners of magic, have been granted the privilege of telling a magical story. A story of love, of honour, of friendship and of betrayal ... A story of King Arthur. A man so mighty and so good that to give an account of such a great man and his exploits will require storytellers of the very finest calibre. Do you consider yourselves worthy of such a task?

> APPRENTICE 2
> We do, my lord, and hold ourselves in readiness.

> MERLIN
> Each of you shall be entrusted with the portrayal of several characters from this wondrous tale. Characters into which you must breathe such vigour and such colour that their lives and yours shall become inseparable. Apprentice 1!

> APPRENTICE 1
> My lord, Merlin!

> MERLIN
> To you I give the characters of the boy Arthur and of the wicked and vengeful Morgan Le Fay.

> APPRENTICE 1
> *(Drops hood)* 'I intend to destroy everything and everyone that King Arthur holds dear.'

> MERLIN
> Apprentice 2!

> APPRENTICE 2
> My lord, Merlin!

> MERLIN
> To you the scheming King Uther, the mysterious Black Knight and Arthur as man and King.

> APPRENTICE 2
>
> (*Drops hood*) 'I shall defend this land and her people with every fibre of my being.'

> MERLIN
>
> Apprentice 3!

> APPRENTICE 3
>
> My lord, Merlin!

> MERLIN
>
> To you the snivelling Sir Kay, and the beautiful and accomplished Queen Guinevere.

> APPRENTICE 3
>
> (*Drops hood*) 'I commit my life to the service of my country as its Queen.'

> MERLIN
>
> Apprentice 4!

> APPRENTICE 4
>
> My lord, Merlin!

> MERLIN
>
> To you the wise Sir Ector, the evil Sir Mordred and the sadly inept Sir Galahad.

> APPRENTICE 4
>
> (*Drops hood, the atmosphere is broken as he grins broadly and we recognize him from pre-show*) Hello!

> MERLIN
>
> To me shall fall the roles of Sir Lancelot, King Arthur's most loyal Knight and, of course, myself — no meagre player in this drama. And so let our story of Arthur, Camelot and the Knights of the Round Table ... begin!!!

2. A ROOM IN THE CASTLE OF KING UTHER

King Uther and Merlin. It is the dead of night, a storm rages outside.

> MERLIN
>
> King Uther, why have you summoned me on such a fearful night as this?

> UTHER
>
> Merlin, you must help me.

> MERLIN
>
> Must I? What is it that you require?

UTHER

I will speak frankly as befits the lateness of the
hour. I am in love with the wife of my greatest and
most hated enemy. I intend to murder him and to make
her mine but I shall require your help.

MERLIN

What do you ask?

UTHER

I ask that you employ your magic to aid me in my
endeavour.

MERLIN

Your endeavour is evil in the extreme. My magic is
reserved for good.

UTHER

Merlin, I am a very rich man ... I would see you well
rewarded for your efforts.

MERLIN

Do you dare to think that the great Merlin, master
magician, can be bought?

UTHER

Forgive me, but I am a desperate man and as a desperate
man I am prepared to compensate you highly for any *com-
promising* of your moral standards.

MERLIN

If I do this thing, I shall demand a price far greater
than gold alone.

UTHER

Name it!

MERLIN

I will do as you request. Your enemy shall die and his
widow enchanted to your favour. You shall be wed but ...

UTHER

Yes?

MERLIN

The bitter fruits of such misdeeds must not be bestowed
upon generations yet unborn. Any child of this union
must be given up to me within a week of birth. I will
entrust them into the safekeeping of a home where they
may grow in truth, honour and justice ... Free from the
taint of evil.

UTHER

This price, high as it is, I am willing to pay.

MERLIN
Then so it shall be done ... and may you, and I, be
forgiven.

Loud thunder clap.

3. A ROOM IN THE CASTLE OF SIR ECTOR

Sir Ector and Merlin. It is daytime, birds sing.

MERLIN
Sir Ector, I must speak with you.

ECTOR
Merlin, is that you, my lord?

MERLIN
Yes it is I. You must listen to what I have to say with
great attention.

ECTOR
I am listening, Merlin.

MERLIN
Within the year I will visit you again. I will bring to
you a child and that child I will give up unto your
safe keeping.

ECTOR
Whom shall this child be?

MERLIN
No questions must you ask but trust in me entirely.

ECTOR
That trust, as always, I shall give.

MERLIN
The child will be a baby boy. You must care for him as
your own, and through the years you must educate him in
the ways of honesty, valour and justice.

ECTOR
If this be your will, then I shall comply.

MERLIN
You must nurture this boy as if he were a rare and ten-
der plant, for one day he will become a great man, who
will bring to you boundless pride. And you shall call
this boy ... Arthur.

4. SOMEWHERE IN ENGLAND

It is a bright morning. A sword protrudes from a stone. Sir Ector and Sir Kay (who is an upper-class idiot).

           ECTOR

It is declared by divine proclamation of the revered Enchanter Merlin, that whosoever draws this sword from the stone shall be the true born King of All Britain.

           KAY

Father, when shall it be my turn to draw that bally sword?

           ECTOR

'Attempt' to draw the sword, my boy, *'attempt'* — you are not King yet, you know.

           KAY

Yes, I know but I'm sure I shall be. I am a brave, true and faithful Knight, aren't I, Father?

           ECTOR

(Hesitantly) Yes, Sir Kay, you are.

           KAY

With strength of mind, body and soul, amply sufficient to surpass all others and claim my true and rightful place as King?

           ECTOR

Perhaps.

           KAY

Well then, let's get on with it. Let me have a go at that old swordy thingy right now. I'm, bound to pull it out first go ... I'm ever so strong ... and then I can start being all Kingly and royal straight away. I've been practising the walk. *(He minces)*

           ECTOR

No, my son, you must wait. Merlin has decreed that each Knight shall have his appointed time to try.

           KAY

Oh Father, don't be so beastly. You know very well that the others don't stand a chance. I'm obviously royal material — I've got the clipped vowel sounds and everything.

           ECTOR

Patience, Sir Kay, patience!

           KAY

And I'm very good with people. I'm the people's King if ever there was one. I'll even go on the road touching lepers if I have to. How's the wave? *(He does a royal wave)*

ECTOR

Perfect, Kay, but premature. Each shall take his turn at the stone. Merlin has spoken.

KAY

Oh Merlin, Merlin, Merlin! That's all we hear nowadays. Everyone's gone Merlin bonkers. I think he's a crank. I mean, all that magic and potions and floating around on a cloud of joy and stuff ... It's very eight hundred and sixties. Too much extract of worzle weed if you ask me!

ECTOR

More respect if you please, young man. Merlin is the great wise magician of our time.

KAY

Rubbish! A proper day's work and a wash wouldn't do him any harm.

ECTOR

Kay!

KAY

Sorry, Father. But when can I draw the sword?

Sir Lancelot enters.

ECTOR

Sir Lancelot is the next. Welcome, Sir Lancelot!

LANCELOT

Thank you, Sir Ector. I am honoured to have been invited. I only hope that I am worthy to try my hand at the sword.

ECTOR

More than worthy.

LANCELOT

Greetings to you, Sir Kay!

KAY

Hello, Lancey. I don't know why you've bothered to show up. I'm going to be King you know.

LANCELOT

(amused) Is that so, Kay?

KAY

Yes! I'm the obvious choice to unite the country.

LANCELOT

Indeed you are. We need a good simple soul, untainted by intellect to cloud his judgement.

                    KAY
Thanks ... I think ... anyway — no hard feelings when
I'm crowned then?

                  LANCELOT
None at all, Kay, none at all.

                    ECTOR
It is time, Sir Lancelot. You must now attempt to draw
the sword. *(He takes Lancelot aside)* Good luck, my
friend. Between you and me, yours is just the kind of
strong and upright character we need at present.

                  LANCELOT
Things are bad, aren't they, Sir Ector?

                    ECTOR
Disastrous! Worse than is generally reported. Civil war
rages in every corner of our land and our enemies from
abroad grow ever more aggressive. The country must
unite if we are to be saved from invasion from without
and turmoil from within. He that can bind us together
and defeat our enemies will be worthy of the title
'King.'

                    KAY
What are you whispering about? Don't you know it's rude
to whisper?

                    ECTOR
Come my friend, the time has come. *(He leads Lancelot
to the stone)*.

                    KAY
Good luck, Lancey!

                  LANCELOT
Thank you, Sir Kay.

                    KAY
You'll need it!

Lancelot tries the sword and fails.

                    KAY
Oh, bad luck, old chap! But I did warn you. You've
either got it or you haven't.

                    ECTOR
Commiserations, Sir Lancelot! I am bitterly disappointed that you are not to be King.

                    KAY
Father! ... what about a bit of loyalty?

                         LANCELOT
     It has been a great honour to have tried. May he who is
     chosen by the Sword live long and prosper.

                         ECTOR
     Amen to that, my friend!

                         KAY
     Thanks, Lancey — I'll do my best.

                         LANCELOT
     Goodbye, Sir Ector and good luck to you Kay.

                         KAY
     Thanks again, old bean, but I won't really need it.
     Don't be too disappointed will you. I'll see you get a
     few jollies when I'm King.

                         ECTOR
     (embarrassed) I'll see you to your horse.

Ector and Lancelot exit.

*Left alone Kay goes to the sword and, after making sure the
coast is clear, tries to pull it out.*

                         KAY
     Bother! It must be stuck.

He tries again.

     Bother! Bother! Bother! Come on you stupid sword. Come
     out. Don't you know who I am? I'm the true-born King of
     all Britain. You're supposed to let me pull you out.

He tries again.

     Please, please come out. Oh please do, Sword — I do so
     want to be King ...... I've got the legs for it.

He tries again.

     Right! That's it! This is your last chance. I'm going
     to count to three and if you don't come out then I'm
     going to thrash you. One, two, three!

He neglects to try this time.

     Very well ... fine! Don't say I didn't warn you.

*He picks up an branch and starts thrashing the stone and
sword. Young Arthur enters.*

                         YA
     What are you doing, Kay?

                              KAY
          (Startled) Nothing!

                              YA
          Why are you hitting that stone? (from his direction of
          approach he can't see the sword).

                              KAY
          Just doing my exercises. (He does some more to cover)
          Got to keep fit if I'm going to be King, you know.

                              YA
          Can I still be your Squire when you're King?

                              KAY
          Don't be stupid! I won't need a Squire when I'm King.
          Kings don't have Squires. Kings have ... well ...
          special Squires and ... things.

                              YA
          Can I be your Special Squire, then?

                              KAY
          No you cannot! I might not even be able to speak to
          you. I'll probably be far too important to consort with
          lowly Squires like you.

                              YA
          But I'm your brother!

                              KAY
          Foster brother! Besides, duty comes before family.

                              YA
          I see!

                              KAY
          By the way, where's my sword? I couldn't find it this
          morning. You didn't put it out for me with my armour.

                              YA
          I couldn't find it either. I thought you had it.

                              KAY
          Brilliant! So now you've lost my sword — some Squire
          you are!

                              YA
          Sorry, Kay!

                              KAY
          Sir Kay if you don't mind. Show some respect, you lit-
          tle brat ..... now go and find my sword at once.

                              YA
          Yes ... Sir Kay! (He exits fast)

                        KAY
    It would be easier to train a monkey!

*He goes to the sword and tries again and again, until he
finally collapses on it and cries bitterly and genuinely.
Ector enters.*

                        ECTOR
    Kay, are you all right?

                        KAY
    (Jumping up) Yes, Father. Just a little tired, that's
    all.

                        ECTOR
    Not *too* tired I hope. Your patience has been reward-
    ed. It is now time for you to attempt to draw the
    Sword.

                        KAY
    Me?

                        ECTOR
    Yes!

                        KAY
    Isn't there anyone else who'd like a go first?

                        ECTOR
    No, it's your turn. A little time ago you couldn't
    wait.

                        KAY
    Yes ... that's right ... I can't wait. But I don't want
    to be selfish. There must be loads of Knights who want
    to have a shot at it.

                        ECTOR
    There are. But it's your time. Your moment to be judged
    is finally here. The Sword will decide if you are the
    one. The right one, fit to rule this mighty land and
    all her people. And you, Sir Kay, are certainly a
    'right one'!

                        KAY
    (Nearly crying again) Oh dear!

                        ECTOR
    What is wrong, my boy? You do want to be King, do you
    not?

                        KAY
    Oh yes, I want to be King more than anything else in
    the whole wide world. And I'd be a wonderful King —
    I've read all the books.

ECTOR
Well, then, step up to the stone.

KAY
No! ... not yet!

ECTOR
But why?

KAY
I'm not ready ... I mean ... I don't want to rush it,
do I?

ECTOR
I know what it is.

KAY
You do?

ECTOR
Yes! You want an audience. You are such a show-off,
Kay. You want your fellow Knights about you when you
make your challenge. I will go to fetch them here.

KAY
NO! Don't do that! They might be busy ... polishing
their armour and sharpening their axes and whatnot ...
I wouldn't want to bother them.

ECTOR
You are a strange boy. What has happened to all that
confidence. Quickly now, I am beginning to lose my
patience. Stand up to the Stone and attempt to draw the
Sword.

KAY
(Losing his temper now) That's right ... bully me as
usual. Do this ... do that ... You've never considered
my feelings. All you care about is honour and chivalry
... but you've never shown me any proper love.

ECTOR
Kay, what are you talking about?

KAY
I'm an adult you know. It's about time you started
treating me like one ... instead of a little boy to be
pushed around. Arthur's always been your favourite ...
and he's not even your proper son. It's all Arthur this
and Arthur that and 'isn't Arthur clever' ... well I'm
fed up with it ... do you hear! I'm sick of doing what
you tell me all the time. I didn't even want to be King
... I wouldn't do it if you paid me ... well I would
get paid, but that's not the point..let Arthur be
King if he's so special ... Arthur King of Britain —
what a joke!

He rushes out.

                    ECTOR
    What did I say? *(following him)* Kay, come back, my boy!

Young Arthur enters.

                    YA
    (Calling) Kay, Kay ... I mean Sir Kay ... where are
    you? Oh dear ... I haven't found his sword yet — he's
    going to kill me. He gets really cross when I get
    things wrong. He thinks I'm an idiot ... he's probably
    right. I'm never going to grow up to be a true, brave
    and faithful Knight like him.

He sees the Sword for the first time.

    What's that? *(He goes to it)* Oh, it's a sword ... a
    beautiful one. It doesn't seem to belong to anyone.
    It's just been left here, stuck in a piece of rock.
    I'll give it to Kay. He's sure to forgive me for losing
    his sword when he sees this one ... it's much better
    than his old thing.

He pulls out the sword easily and exits saying:

    Sir Kay, Sir Kay ... where are you?

Kay enters followed by Ector.

                    KAY
    Please leave me alone, Father.

                    ECTOR
    But, Kay, I don't know what is wrong with you. Why are
    you so upset?

                    KAY
    I am not upset. I just don't want to be King anymore,
    that's all ... I could be, if I wanted to, of course
    ... but I don't. So Britain will have to make do with
    second best. I'm sorry but I'm no longer available. The
    people will be disappointed but it's a tough old world.

                    ECTOR
    (He has seen the empty stone) The Sword — it is gone.
    Kay, quickly ... look, it has vanished.

                    KAY
    Well, it was here just now. I felt ... I mean saw it.

                    ECTOR
    The sacred Sword of Judgement entrusted to my care by
    the mighty Merlin — and I have lost it.

                        KAY
You should have kept your eye on it.

                        ECTOR
I would have done if I hadn't been chasing after you.
You and your stupid moods.

                        KAY
Well I like that! I don't have moods. I'm just sensitive, that's all. And strong of course. I'm the strong,
sensitive type.

                        ECTOR
You're the pathetic, stupid type.

                        KAY
Father!

                        ECTOR
Oh, shut up, Kay. What am I going to do? I have been
honoured with the highest of responsibilities by Merlin
and I have let him down.

                        KAY
Priest-holes to Merlin! Who gives a Knight's nuptials
what he thinks, anyhow! Anyway, how could the sword
have gone? Nobody could pull it out. It was stuck fast
... I should imagine.

                        ECTOR
Nobody but the true born King of Britain.

Enter Young Arthur with the sword.

                        YA
Kay! There you are! I've been looking for you every-
where. I haven't found your sword I'm afraid. I'm really sorry. I know I'm an idiot but don't be cross with
me. I've found you another one. It's much nicer than
yours. Here it is. Isn't it beautiful?

He gives the sword to Kay who screams and drops it.

                        ECTOR
(In shock) Arthur, where did you get that sword?

                        YA
I found it — over there, Father. It was stuck in that
rock. Have I done wrong? It wasn't really stealing — it
had just been left there.

                        ECTOR
No, Arthur, you haven't done wrong. But show me how you
took the sword.

YA

Pardon, Father?

ECTOR

Put the sword back into the rock where you found it and then show me how you pulled it out.

YA

Very well, Father.

He puts it in the stone.

It was just like this. I saw it and I just ... took it ... like this.

He does so.

Merlin appears and Ector and Kay fall to their knees.

5. THE LAKE

MERLIN

Arthur, you are the chosen one. To you is given this day all majesty and power. Upon your head shall be placed the crown and you shall become the almighty ruler of this land. But be not proud, for to you falls a most difficult and dangerous quest. You are to find unity and peace for this country. The search will be hard and you will face many dangers. There will be those who will lose faith with you, those who will hate you and those who will try to do you harm. But fear not, for yours is a just quest. A quest that will restore this great kingdom to its rightful place of glory in this world. And you will not be alone, for I will always be here, never far from your side ... ever ready to guide you along the treacherous path that you must take. Also, to you will be given a sword. A great and mighty sword — far mightier than that which you drew from the stone. With this sword you will conquer all your foes and rule with truth, honour and justice. Come — let me take you to the keeper of this sword. Across the Lake of Dreams you must go. Look down, deep down, into the very waters of life and you will see the Lady of the Lake. She will not speak, nor take your hand — but the water itself will call your name and she will hand to you the Sword ... Excalibur!

A boat has appeared. Arthur rows onto the lake. The Lady of the Lake emerges from the water and hands him Excalibur.

And now you must begin your reign. You must start off along the road that has been chosen for you. Go carefully — there are many turnings along the route which you must not take and many travelling companions of whom you must beware. But there will be many good times

too and many, many friends. And as you journey you will
become a legend. Arthur the boy will grow into Arthur
the man — the true-born King of all Britain.

*We see Arthur transform from boy to man. He holds Excalibur
aloft as the scene ends.*

6. CAMELOT

            MERLIN
And so began the greatest chapter of our history.
Arthur was a wonderful King and under his firm leadership Britain began to unite and defend herself against
the many threats from overseas. In time, Arthur fell in
love with the beautiful Guinevere, daughter of one of
his most faithful subjects. They were married and set
up home in the majestic castle, Camelot that was especially built by Arthur to be his kingdom within a kingdom, centre of a now mighty country.

Arthur and Guinevere enter.

            ARTHUR
What are you thinking about, my love?

            GUINEVERE
How wonderful this place is. How lucky I am. How happy.
Those kind of thoughts.

            ARTHUR
Ah! — those kinds of thoughts. You know, ever since I was a
boy I have dreamed of this place. I built it in my mind a
thousand times. Camelot — home to a great and mighty King!

            GUINEVERE
And now you are that King and this Camelot is real and
not a dream.

            ARTHUR
I still think I'm dreaming when I look at you.

            MERLIN
To this Camelot King Arthur brought a band of brave and
trusted knights. Men upon whom he could rely in good
times and in bad. These knights became known throughout
the land for their chivalry and honour. Each had his
place around a great table. Each was equal. Each served
each other. And each would gladly die for the rest. They
were called the Knights of the Round Table; you may have
heard of them. As well as these knights there was a
group of other knights — less noble in stature but
equally brave. These knights were not all men but women
and children too. People of all ages, forgotten by the
storybooks, but who were just as loyal to the King. They
were called the Knights Auditoria.

MERLIN, ARTHUR AND GUINEVERE
(pointing to audience) Long live the Knights Auditoria!

MERLIN
And so stood Camelot.

ARTHUR

May God bless this Kingdom and all her loyal subjects!

MERLIN
The Knights of the Round Table replied:

KNIGHTS
(On tape) Long live King Arthur!

MERLIN
And this was echoed by the Knights Auditoria:

AUDIENCE
Long live King Arthur! *(Merlin cajoles them until they say this)*

MERLIN
Oh ... and then there was Sir Galahad!

All exit as Sir Galahad enters.

GALAHAD
Long Live King Arthur! Hello ... you're the Knights Auditoria aren't you? ... thought so. Sorry! It's just when you're at Round Table level you don't see much of the lesser Knights. Oh, sorry — that sounded snobbish, didn't it? I didn't mean it to come out like that. I'm always saying things I don't mean — it's a habit. I've got nothing to be snobbish about, anyway. I'm only on the Round Table because of me name — Sir Galahad. I'm supposed to be all gallant and sophisticated and good with women. Trouble is I have a bit of a job living up to my legend. Actually I'm not like that at all ... in fact, I'm a bit of an idiot really. I can't seem to get anything right. I put my armour on the wrong way round ..... when I swing my sword savagely round me head I fall off me horse ... I tuck me tabard into me under-pants. If I'm sent out to slay an hoard of marauding invaders, I usually get the wrong ones. Last week I attacked the Second Camelot Scout Troop ... well, they looked pretty vicious to me! I'm not very good at fighting at all really. You see, I'm not very brave ... I'm supposed to be ... but I'm not. Sometimes when we go into battle I shake so much the visor on me helmet rattles. Well it's not easy taking on these hard fight-ing, pillaging, barbarous, marauding, Knight slayers ... some of them are quite rough, you know!

Arthur enters.

ARTHUR
Sir Galahad!

GALAHAD
It's the King. Yes, Your Majesty!

ARTHUR
I've got a job for you.

GALAHAD
A job for me? Isn't there someone else you'd rather do
it?

ARTHUR
No, Sir Galahad. I want you to do it. I wish you to ride
out beyond the gates. A lady of high birth has expressed
a wish to visit us and witness Camelot at first hand.
You will intercept her on her journey and escort her
here with all the solemnity belonging to her station.

GALAHAD
Are you sure I'm the right man for the job?

ARTHUR
Quite sure! After all, you do have a reputation for a
certain way with the ladies.

GALAHAD
I know I do, Your Majesty, but it's not true. I come
over all unnecessary when I talk to a woman. I shake
more than I do when I'm going into battle.

ARTHUR
Come, come, Sir Galahad — enough of your false modesty.
Away with you now and charm her.

Arthur exits.

GALAHAD
Oh hec! I've been given a special job. Fancy that!
Picked by the King to charm a lady of high standing.
Chosen because of my cool, sophisticated way with women
.... I'd better go and change me socks!

He goes to exit but meets Guinevere as she enters.

GUINEVERE
Sir Galahad, have you seen my husband?

GALAHAD
Yes he was here but a moment ago, Your Majesty. Shall I
find him for you?

GUINEVERE
No, please don't trouble yourself. I am sure I can find
him.

GALAHAD
Thank you very much, Your Majesty. You're very gra-
cious, Your Majesty.

GUINEVERE
Are you all right, Sir Galahad. You seem a little agi-
tated.

GALAHAD
Well you see, Your Majesty ...

GUINEVERE
Please call me Guinevere.

GALAHAD
Oh hec!... Guinevere ... I've been chosen to meet and
greet a very important lady visitor.

GUINEVERE
I see! What is her name?

GALAHAD
What is her name?

GUINEVERE
Yes!

GALAHAD
Oh hec!... King Arthur!... King Arthur!

*He rushes off. Guinevere laughs. Arthur enters from another
direction, creeps up on her and puts his hands over her eyes.*

ARTHUR
Guess who?

GUINEVERE
Um ... now let me think ... Sir Kay?

ARTHUR
(Spinning her around to him) Sir Kay indeed! And what
do you know of Sir Kay?

GUINEVERE
Only that he's extremely handsome.

ARTHUR
He's a pompous idiot!

GUINEVERE
He's your brother.

ARTHUR
Foster brother, as he was once so keen to remind me.

> GUINEVERE
> I've been looking for you.

> ARTHUR
> Have you indeed! *(He tries to kiss her)*

> GUINEVERE
> Stop it, Arthur ... someone might see.

> ARTHUR
> Let them! *(he kisses her)* Now, what do you want to talk to me about?

> GUINEVERE
> Do you know, I've quite forgotten. *(She kisses him)*

Sir Lancelot enters.

> LANCELOT
> Your Majesty ... oh, sorry sire ... I'll come back later.

> GUINEVERE
> It's all right, Sir Lancelot. My husband can talk to you. I must get on anyway — I have much to attend to.

> LANCELOT
> *(Bowing to her)* Your Majesty!

She exits.

> ARTHUR
> You look worried, Sir Lancelot. It is unlike you to seem so serious on such a sunny day. What troubles you?

> LANCELOT
> I'm not sure, your majesty ... I may be mistaken.

> ARTHUR
> My friend, you have become my most loyal and trusted knight. I feel that I know you better than any other man. You are rarely mistaken about anything. Now come, spit it out, Sir. What is wrong?

> LANCELOT
> Arthur, I sense that you are in danger.

> ARTHUR
> I am always in danger. My quest to unite Britain and make her strong again has been nothing but perilous. To be King is never to be safe.

> LANCELOT
> This is a different kind of danger. A danger from within. I understand a lady of noble birth is to visit Camelot.

146

ARTHUR

Indeed ... a lady called Morgan Le Fay ... I've just
sent Sir Galahad to meet her at the gates.

LANCELOT

Don't trust her, Arthur. I have heard rumours about
her. Suspicion surrounds her like a cloak.

ARTHUR

What exactly have you heard?

LANCELOT

Nothing in particular, just that she is a schemer and
manipulator, and that she will stop at nothing in order
to get her way.

ARTHUR

Who has said this about her?

LANCELOT

Nobody in particular ... it's just what I have heard.

ARTHUR

No facts in particular from nobody in particular ...
Could it be that you are prejudging her, my friend?

LANCELOT

Perhaps, but.

ARTHUR

Then *perhaps* we should wait and see for ourselves.

LANCELOT

Yes, Sire!

ARTHUR

I appreciate your concern, Sir Lancelot, and I will
bear it in mind ... I promise. If she asks me to lend
her money I shall refuse.

LANCELOT

You are mocking me, your majesty.

ARTHUR

Not at all. I value your advice. But at present I have
far greater worries to occupy my mind. The evil Sir
Mordred has raised an army and threatens us from the
west.

LANCELOT

I thought that Mordred was a broken man since we last
defeated him.

ARTHUR
Mordred is a survivor. Evil can repair itself with
lightning speed. I hear that he now has some twenty
thousand men at his command. He is a man who will stop
at nothing to achieve his ends. Rarely have I met such
arrogance, such cruelty, such disregard for human life.
Oh, pity this poor country should it ever fall into the
hands of one so deplorable as he. He intends to take
the crown from me by force.

LANCELOT
Then this is grave news indeed.

ARTHUR
Fear not, Sir Lancelot. Camelot's walls and our hearts
will stand against the mightiest of foes. When the time
comes we will be ready. Now come ... no more talk of
rumours and suspicions, we must greet our most honoured
guest.

Sound of trumpets.

Enter Sir Galahad with Morgan Le Fay.

GALAHAD
Presenting her highly upper crustiness, the majestic
noble personage — Morgan Leafy.

MORGAN
(In a whisper to him) Le Fay!

GALAHAD
Bless you!

ARTHUR
Morgan Le Fay, welcome to Camelot.

MORGAN
(curtseying) King Arthur, I am honoured to meet you,
Your Majesty.

ARTHUR
I am delighted and flattered by your interest in
Camelot. I hope that you enjoy your stay with us.

MORGAN
Who wouldn't be interested in such a place? And may I
say, at the risk of embarrassing Your Majesty, that its
magnificence is entirely suitable for such a King as
you.

ARTHUR
Thank you.

MORGAN

I so very much admire what you have done for this country. This land has waited long for the strength and
resolve that you have bestowed upon it.

ARTHUR

You are too kind.

MORGAN

Strength and resolve are two qualities that I find very
becoming in a man.

Guinevere and Lancelot enter.

ARTHUR

Morgan, allow me to introduce you to my wife, Queen
Guinevere.

GUINEVERE

It is extremely kind of you to visit us.

MORGAN

The kindness is yours in allowing me to do so, Your
Majesty.

GUINEVERE

I do hope that you will be comfortable.

MORGAN

I am sure I shall. Perhaps you would allow me to say
how fortunate you are to be the Queen of such an imposing and powerful King.

GUINEVERE

I count myself fortunate indeed. And now, if you will
excuse me, I must see to the preparation of your cham-
bers.

She exits.

ARTHUR

Would you like to be shown around Camelot, Morgan? I
warn you — there is much to see.

MORGAN

That would be wonderful. How grand — to be taken upon a
guided tour by the King himself!

ARTHUR

Alas, no, I am afraid that I have much to attend to.
But allow me to present Sir Lancelot. He will escort
you in my stead.

LANCELOT

(Stepping forward) Greetings, madam!

MORGAN
Charmed, I'm sure!

ARTHUR
Sir Lancelot knows as much about Camelot as I do
myself. More perhaps. For my part, I look forward to
seeing you at dinner.

MORGAN
Your Majesty!

She curtseys as he exits.

MORGAN
So, you are the famous Sir Lancelot. I have heard a
very great deal about you. The King's most loyal and
trusted friend, so I believe.

LANCELOT
I flatter myself that I do indeed enjoy His Majesty's
favour.

MORGAN
You're very formal, Sir Lancelot. Do I intimidate you?

LANCELOT
No, madam. Why should you?

MORGAN
Why should I indeed! Perhaps you don't like me.

LANCELOT
I think nothing of you, we have only just met.

MORGAN
You think nothing of me? Most men fall at my feet the
very first time they set eyes upon me. Do you not find
me attractive, Sir Lancelot?

LANCELOT
The King has instructed me to accompany you on a tour
of the castle.

MORGAN
There's plenty of time for that later. I think we
should get to know each other a little first. I won't
eat you, you know. Loosen up a little ... I'm really
very nice ... when you get to know me properly.

LANCELOT
I don't doubt it.

MORGAN
Oh but, Sir Lancelot, I think you do. I think you doubt
it very much. But, no matter! Let me ask your opinion
of something. I have brought some fine wine to grace

the King's table. Perhaps you would sample it for me ... to ensure that you feel it suitable for the royal palate.

                    LANCELOT
I will do so with pleasure, Madam.

                    MORGAN
Splendid! I can see how the King values your service so. I am sure he would be quite devastated to lose you.

                    LANCELOT
Perhaps!

                    MORGAN
Perhaps? ... I am certain of it. I feel sure that without you a very large piece of his perfect world would crumble. Here, take this. *(hands him a tumbler of wine)* Your very good health! Now, isn't this cosy ... the sun beginning to set, the mighty vista of Camelot spread before us, and a drink shared ... what could be more romantic?

                    LANCELOT
The wine has a fine texture ... and yet.

                    MORGAN
Is there something wrong, Sir Lancelot?

                    LANCELOT
No, I think not ... the smell of the wine is a little strong, that is all.

                    MORGAN
But its taste is divine, I assure you. Now, drink up or I shall be offended.

                    LANCELOT
Forgive me but I have some urgent business to attend to.

                    MORGAN
But your drink ... you haven't touched it.

                    LANCELOT
Later perhaps, I really must go. The King requires my attendance. I will see you at dinner. *(he exits)*

                    MORGAN
Away then. Run to the King like the puppy-dog that you are. Attend the King while you can. For it is my intention to destroy the King as he destroyed me. I will take from him every little part of his honourable existence. I will take his friends, his happiness, his precious Camelot ... and finally, I will take his life.

Sound of distant thunder.

The poor fool has no idea who I really am. To him I'm
just one more guest to politely entertain. He will know
nothing of a small child who stood in the shadows and
watched his father kill mine ... nothing of how that
child's life was ruined before it had properly begun
... nothing of the pain his half-sister has endured
watching him become the richest and most powerful man
in the world. Oh yes — I will kill him, but first I
will hurt him. And I know exactly how ... for to lose
one particular thing would hurt him more than losing
everything else put together. Sir Lancelot can wait ...
I must away to find my hostess, Queen Guinevere.

Thunder swells as she exits.

It is a new day, Galahad and Arthur enter from opposite sides.

ARTHUR

Sir Galahad!

GALAHAD

Yes, Sire?

ARTHUR

Have you seen the Queen?

GALAHAD

No Sire, she's out for the day.

ARTHUR

Out?

GALAHAD

Yes! She rode out with the Lady Morgan early this morn-
ing. Lady Morgan has taken the Queen to see her own
Castle .... repaying the hospitality, she said.
They'll be gone all day.

ARTHUR

I see! Thank you Sir Galahad!

He exits.

GALAHAD

You're welcome, Sire! Hello, Knights Auditoria. Did you
hear that. The King relies on me, you know. I'm his
right-hand man. Only the other day I heard him say that
Camelot would be a completely different place without
me. He did. I think I'm finally beginning to live up to
my name. With your help.

7. MORGAN'S CASTLE

Morgan and Guinevere.

> MORGAN
>
> Well, Your Majesty, what do you think of my humble
> abode? Not as grand as Camelot, of course, but a worthy
> Castle — would you agree?

> GUINEVERE
>
> (*Hesitantly*) Yes ... quite worthy ... just a little
> gloomy perhaps.

> MORGAN
>
> Gloomy?

> GUINEVERE
>
> It does seem to be a little overgrown.

> MORGAN
>
> Yes ... I see what you mean. The forest has invaded a
> little since I was last here. I'm so seldom home, you
> see. I'm in such demand, socially.

> GUINEVERE
>
> Do you not have servants?

> MORGAN
>
> But of course ... normally ... it's just so difficult
> to find staff these days.

> GUINEVERE
>
> (*Increasingly uneasy*) Morgan, why have you brought me
> here?

> MORGAN
>
> I thought that you would like to see my home. Of
> course, if you don't like it.

> GUINEVERE
>
> I did not mean to offend you. I'm sorry.

> MORGAN
>
> Your Majesty, it is I who should apologize. You see, I
> do have another reason for bringing you here.

> GUINEVERE
>
> You do?

> MORGAN
>
> Yes. I wanted to talk to you. In private.

> GUINEVERE
>
> What about?

MORGAN
Oh dear! I fear that it will be a little difficult.

GUINEVERE
What do you have to say, Morgan?

MORGAN
It's about your husband.

GUINEVERE
My husband?

MORGAN
Yes. There is something I think you should know.

GUINEVERE
What?

MORGAN
Well, the truth is ...... your Majesty .... oh, this
is so hard for me to say .....

GUINEVERE
Delay no further. Say what you have to say.

MORGAN
King Arthur has been very friendly towards me.

GUINEVERE
King Arthur is always friendly towards his guests.

MORGAN
But to me he has been *particularly* friendly. In fact, I
fear to tell, that he has tried to win my favour.

GUINEVERE
Nonsense!

MORGAN
At first I thought it was my imagination. But upon discussion with other ladies of the Court, I find that
they too have been unduly flattered by him.

GUINEVERE
I don't believe it. You must be mistaken. King Arthur's
manner is entirely proper with all ladies.

MORGAN
When you are present perhaps ... but when you are not
... well, apparently his attentions are less than
proper.

GUINEVERE
Morgan, you are a liar! You are trying to poison my
mind against Arthur.

> MORGAN
> But why should I do that?

> GUINEVERE
> I don't know, but you are. I am beginning to think that
> Sir Lancelot was right. He told me that you were not to
> be trusted, that you were out to make trouble ... and
> so, it seems, you are.

> MORGAN
> Lancelot is a fool! You think me a liar because you
> can't face the fact that your precious Arthur isn't the
> honourable man every one of his simpering subjects seem
> to think he is.

> GUINEVERE
> Why do you hate him so?

> MORGAN
> I don't. I just know him for what he is, that's all.

> GUINEVERE
> I refuse to listen to another word of this.

She makes to exit.

> MORGAN
> Wait!

Guinevere turns.

> MORGAN
> By the power of all magic ever known, may royal flesh
> be turned to stone.

Guinevere freezes.

> So what if they are lies, my sweet. More fool you for
> not believing them, for the truth is far worse.

Merlin enters.

> MERLIN
> Morgan!

> MORGAN
> Why! — the great enchanter himself. How wonderful to
> see you, Merlin.

> MERLIN
> Morgan, why are you doing this?

> MORGAN
> You know why, old man.

MERLIN

I know that you are using your magic for bad things.

MORGAN

Something that you would never do, of course. Except you did, didn't you? Many years ago.

MERLIN

I do not understand your words.

MORGAN

Don't you? Well, let me tell you a story and see if it rings any bells for you. Once upon a time, there was a rich King called Uther who fell in love with a beautiful woman. But although this King had many things, this woman he could not have for she was married and, besides, she did not return his love. So Uther, undeterred, enlisted the help of a magician — the greatest of his day — and with this sorcerer's assistance a nobleman died and his widow was, mysteriously, remarried within a week. And that magician was you.

MERLIN

This was all a very long time ago.

MORGAN

Merlin — the kind and wise — isn't that how you are thought of. But we know different, don't we?

MERLIN

I have made amends for my sin.

MORGAN

Uther and his new Queen had a baby boy. A boy who, with your help, was to follow in his murdering father's Kingly footsteps.

MERLIN

I have watched over him and protected him.

MORGAN

But this Queen already had a child. A small girl. Did you watch over her? Did you protect her? Obviously not, for all she has now is this stinking ruin of a castle.

MERLIN

You have always been very good at looking after yourself, Morgan.

MORGAN

All I have now is my magic and this pathetic reminder of a once magnificent royal castle. But, for my purposes now, they will be enough.

MERLIN

What are you going to do?

                        MORGAN
I'm going to make him pay for his father's crime —
that's what I'm going to do.

                        MERLIN
But he's your half-brother.

                        MORGAN
Forgive me but my family loyalty is at an all-time low. Oh,
by the way — I do hope you won't think of telling tales on
me. Otherwise, I might just have to tell tales on you.

INTERVAL

8. A ROOM AT CAMELOT

Merlin and Arthur.

                        MERLIN
Arthur!

                        ARTHUR
Merlin, is that you?

                        MERLIN
Yes, my boy, it is.

                        ARTHUR
All my life you have appeared when I need you most.
Merlin, I am so worried. The threat from Mordred grows
stronger day by day — I hear tell that he is preparing
to march upon Camelot. And now Guinevere is late in
returning home.

                        MERLIN
I see that worry for your wife takes second place in
your thoughts.

                        ARTHUR
Do not judge me, Merlin. I am King. My duty must come
first. Isn't that what you have always taught me?

                        MERLIN
Yes, my friend, it is — but you must hurry to the aid
of Guinevere immediately as she is in grave danger.

                        ARTHUR
You know where she is? Tell me!

                        MERLIN
She is imprisoned in Morgan's castle. Turned to stone
by an evil magic. You must make haste to rescue her.

                        ARTHUR
But who has done this? And where is Morgan? Has she
been imprisoned too?

MERLIN
I can say no more. You must move quickly.

ARTHUR
But I cannot leave Camelot; news arrives upon every
hour. I must remain here when such a menace threatens.
If Camelot is lost then the whole of Britain will be
conquered by this evil Mordred. Merlin, can you not use
your magic to rescue her?

MERLIN
No, my boy, alas I cannot.

ARTHUR
But why?

MERLIN
This magic goes deep, Arthur. Very deep — deeper than I
can hope to fathom.

ARTHUR
But you are the most powerful magician that has ever
lived. There is something strange about all of this —
something that you are not telling me, Merlin. What is
it?

MERLIN
There is no time for more talk. You must act. If you
cannot go yourself, then send your best Knights. But do
it now, Arthur, before it is too late.

Merlin exits.

ARTHUR
(Calling) Sir Galahad!

GALAHAD
Enters running.

GALAHAD
Yes, your majesty!

ARTHUR
I have a job for you. A mission of the utmost urgency.

GALAHAD
Oh hec!

ARTHUR
Find Sir Lancelot and go together to Morgan Le Fay's
Castle. There you will find Queen Guinevere in mortal
danger. You must rescue her. Go quickly now — there is
no time to be lost.

GALAHAD
Oh hec! Now I'm really going to have to be brave.

9. BACK AT MORGAN'S CASTLE

Morgan and Guinevere (still frozen).

>   MORGAN
> How are you, my dear? So sorry about the heating in
> here. I'm sure you must be frozen stiff *(laughs)*. I
> imagine you're wondering why I haven't killed you yet.
> Quite simple — I am expecting King Arthur at any
> minute. That pathetic Merlin is sure to have gone
> straight to him and he'll come rushing to the rescue of
> his damsel in distress. And when he arrives, I will
> kill you both. You see, I really am a very wicked lady.

Enter Lancelot and Galahad.

>   LANCELOT
> Morgan! Are you all right? What has happened?

>   MORGAN
> You! Where is King Arthur?

>   LANCELOT
> At Camelot. He has sent us here to rescue Queen
> Guinevere.

>   MORGAN
> She has been turned to stone by an evil magic. I fear
> that she may never be restored to life.

>   GALAHAD
> She looks very cold and pale. Can you hear me, Your
> Majesty? Can you move?

>   MORGAN
> Of course she can't move, you fool, she's turned to
> stone.

>   LANCELOT
> Was this your doing, Morgan?

>   MORGAN
> Mine? Why, of course not. The castle was invaded by the
> Black Knight. Have you heard of him?

>   LANCELOT
> A magical, mythical Knight whose identity has never
> been revealed and who has never been defeated in single
> combat by any other swordsman.

>   MORGAN
> I think he must have followed us here in order to
> attack Queen Guinevere.

>   LANCELOT
> No, Morgan. This is not the work of the Black Knight or

any other Knight. This is your doing. I don't know why you consider King Arthur your enemy but I know that you are intent to harm him and those close to him. I believe you even tried to kill me.

> MORGAN
> Oh, Lancelot — how could you say such a thing? Now I really am hurt. Surely you don't believe that little old me could do a manly Knight any harm. What about you, Galahad. You trust me don't you? A big, strong, sensitive man like you must realize I'm just a harmless pussycat.

She runs her fingers through his hair as she speaks.

> GALAHAD
> Oh hec!

> LANCELOT
> Your game is over, Morgan. Restore Guinevere to life before I forget that I am a gentleman.

> MORGAN
> My, my — the dog bites! Yes very well it was me and, yes, I am Arthur's enemy — though the fool doesn't know it. But the game isn't over. Not yet. In fact it's only just beginning.
> > With magic deep inside of me
> > I create an enemy you can't see
> > With power many times divisible
> > Summon I the Knight Invisible.

A sword (held by the Invisible Knight) appears in mid-air.

> LANCELOT
> Stand back, Sir Galahad. Leave this to me.

> GALAHAD
> Delighted!

Lancelot fights and beats the Invisible Knight.

> GALAHAD
> Well done, Lancelot. I've heard of sword fighting but never fighting a sword.

> MORGAN
> Well done indeed. Nobly fought.

> LANCELOT
> Spare your words, Morgan. Release Guinevere from your wicked spell at once.

> MORGAN
> But the fun isn't over yet. I've another friend for you to meet. You see, when I said that the Black Knight was

here I was telling the truth.
>   I raise my powers to their full height
>   Come my servant. Attend, Black Knight.

The Black Knight appears.

                    GALAHAD
Oh hec! Not again! I know ... stand aside, leave it to
you.

Lancelot fights the Black Knight. It ends with Galahad hitting
the BK on the head.

                    LANCELOT
Thank you, Sir Galahad. Well struck!

                    GALAHAD
I don't know me own strength.

                    LANCELOT
And now, Morgan, if you please.

Both Knights approach her.

                    MORGAN
Stop right there!
>   With crawling hate and creeping vice
>   Knightly vigour, turn to ice.

Both Knights are frozen like Guinevere.

                    MORGAN
You poor little Knights. All that nasty fighting for
nothing. Merlin! Attend me at once, I command you!

                    MERLIN ON TAPE
Morgan, this evil must stop.

                    MORGAN
But, Merlin, my dear, I'm just starting to enjoy
myself. I am disappointed, of course, not to have
snared King Arthur in my trap but the fortuitous
arrival of Sir Lancelot has given me an idea. I intend
to cast my most wicked spell ever. Under my enchantment
Guinevere and Lancelot will fall in love ... and that
will break the King's heart. Of course, I require your
silence but then likewise do you require mine. It would
be so unfortunate for you if your involvement in my
Father's death were to become public knowledge. Not
good for the image. I think we understand each other.
>   Descend upon us from above
>   Oh spirits of eternal love
>   As two shall long to fondly kiss
>   All three forget my part this.

She exits as the others come back to life.

GUINEVERE
Sir Lancelot! Sir Galahad! ... what has happened? What
are you doing here?

GALAHAD
I'm not quite sure. Oh hec! ... I've got cramp!

LANCELOT
Are you all right, Your Majesty?

GUINEVERE
Yes ... At least, I think so. But I'm not sure what's
been going on.

LANCELOT
We were sent to rescue you ... we arrived at the castle
... and then ... it's no use — I can't seem to remember.

GALAHAD
My mind's a blank too. But then, it usually is.

GUINEVERE
Where is Morgan? Have you seen her?

LANCELOT
No ... I don't think so ... I'm not sure.

GUINEVERE
She must have returned to Camelot. But how strange that
she should leave without me.

LANCELOT
The most important thing is that you are safe.

GUINEVERE
Sir Lancelot, I will be eternally grateful to you for
coming to my assistance.

LANCELOT
Think nothing of it, Your Majesty.

GALAHAD
Will you be eternally grateful to me too?

GUINEVERE
You know, Sir Lancelot, how I have always valued highly
your loyalty and friendship. Being Queen can be so lonely
sometimes. I feel that you are the one person who really
understands me ..... the one person I can talk to.

GALAHAD
Don't mind me, will you!

LANCELOT
I will always be your faithful servant, Your Majesty.
You see, I have long been an admirer of yours.

GUINEVERE
Really? How strange! I have always thought very highly
of you too ... very highly indeed.

They make to kiss but Galahad moves swiftly between them.

GALAHAD
Ummm! ... I think we ought to be getting back. The King
will be anxious.

LANCELOT
Quite right, Sir Galahad! Come, Your Majesty. Please
take my arm.

GUINEVERE
Thank you, Lancelot. And please do call me Guinevere.

They all exit, Galahad last as he turns to the audience:

GALAHAD
Oh hec!

10. BACK AT CAMELOT

MERLIN ON TAPE
And so they returned to Camelot. King Arthur was, of
course, delighted to see Guinevere safely home. But, as
time passed, rumours began to spread — rumours, whis-
pered about the court, that told of a liaison between
the Queen and Arthur's most trusted Knight. Guilty in
my silence, I did nothing to intervene and so the
King's mind was turned against his Queen, just as Morgan had intended.

Arthur paces alone. Lancelot enters.

LANCELOT
You wanted to see me, Sire?

ARTHUR
Yes, Sir Lancelot. Please forgive my frankness but,
with Mordred's army moving ever closer, I have little
time. ... I hear tell that you and my wife have, of
late, taken every opportunity to be in each others company ... in fact, that you are in love.

LANCELOT
My Lord, I cannot lie to you. It is true. Please
believe that neither Guinevere nor I intended this to
happen but, to our shame, almost against our will, it
has.

ARTHUR
Sir Lancelot, I have trusted you above all others. How
could you betray me so?

                    LANCELOT
I stand guilty without excuse and humbly await your
punishment.

                    ARTHUR
Your punishment is banishment. I wish you to leave
Camelot at once and never return.

                    LANCELOT
As painful as it will be for me to leave, I will obey.
Please know, Arthur, that it was never my intention to
hurt you.

                    ARTHUR
Get out of my sight!

                    LANCELOT
Your Majesty.

                    ARTHUR
Now!

Lancelot exits.

                    MERLIN ON TAPE
So, Sir Lancelot left Camelot in disgrace and, tormented
by guilt, he took refuge in a monastery, taking the
sacred vows of a monk. But rumours continued to surround
Guinevere. It was said that she had enchanted Sir
Lancelot by evil magic and that she was a witch. Arthur,
his mind and judgement clouded by pain, slowly began to
believe that this was true until, finally, he turned
completely against his beloved wife and sentenced her to
be burnt to death as a witch. And every night I had the
same dream, in which Morgan Le Fay would come to me:

Morgan enters.

                    MORGAN
Merlin, my dear. Everyone thinks that you are such a
wise and wonderful magician, don't they? But you and I
know a different story. We know that you are just as
weak, just as pathetic, just as wicked as the rest of
us ... and thus you are powerless to help dear Guinevere. My plan has worked perfectly ... Guinevere, the
King's precious wife, will be destroyed by his own
hand. *(She laughs)*

She exits and Galahad enters.

                    GALAHAD
Hello, Knights Auditoria! I'm ever so upset, you know.
I've just heard some terrible news. Guinevere is to die
at the stake ... I can't bear it! ... she's such a
lovely lady really. I know she got all over friendly

like with Sir Lancelot ... but I'm sure she didn't mean
to. I don't think she could help it, you know. I've got
this funny feeling that Lady Morgan had something to do
with it all ... but I just can't remember why. Oh well,
I must get on — I've got to build the bonfire ... what
a horrible job — I don't think I can face it!

*Guinevere is tied to the stake. Arthur, Morgan and Galahad are
present.*

                    ARTHUR
Queen Guinevere, have you any last words?

                    GUINEVERE
Yes, I have. Arthur, I have always loved you. I do not
know why my heart turned, as it did, to Lancelot. It
was almost as if I couldn't control my own feelings.
But of one thing I am sure. I regret bitterly the pain
that I have caused you. I do not fear death ... only
the fact that I shall die knowing that you hate me.

                    ARTHUR
Sir Galahad, begin the execution.

                    GALAHAD
I can't, Your Majesty!

                    ARTHUR
Why?

                    GALAHAD
Me taper's damp.

                    ARTHUR
Sir Galahad.

                    GALAHAD
This is a smoke-free zone — we might get in trouble
with the council.

                    ARTHUR
Sir Galahad.

                    GALAHAD
I don't like bright light, it gives me a headache.

                    ARTHUR
SIR GALAHAD!

                    GALAHAD
Oh hec! *(He closes his eyes and holds a match over the
bonfire, thus he remains throughout the following:)* I
really don't want to do this, you know.

Lancelot enters dressed as a monk.

                    LANCELOT
Stop!

                    ARTHUR
Lancelot, is that you? How dare you enter the walls of
Camelot against my wishes.

                    LANCELOT
Please hear me, Your Majesty. You must attend to what I
have to say before it is too late.

                    ARTHUR
There is nothing you can say, Sir Lancelot, that will
make me change my mind. Guinevere must die as a witch.

                    LANCELOT
Guinevere is no witch. There is your witch. *(He points
to Morgan)* Morgan is responsible for everything that
has happened.

                    ARTHUR
What mean you, Sir?

                    MORGAN
Don't listen to him, Your Majesty. Banishment has
obviously driven him mad.

                    LANCELOT
Yes do listen to me, Arthur. I am not mad. Please
believe what I am about to tell you. It was Morgan who
imprisoned Guinevere and when Galahad and I went to
rescue her, it was Morgan who used wicked magic to make
us fall in love.

                    GALAHAD
That's not right! No offence, Lancelot — I've always
been very fond of you, but it's not love.

                    LANCELOT
Not you and me, you idiot! She made Guinevere fall in
love with me and I with her.

                    GALAHAD
Oh, I see what you mean ... you had me worried there.

                    MORGAN
This is all lies, Your Majesty.

                    LANCELOT
It is you who are the liar, Morgan.

                    ARTHUR
If this were true, why would Morgan do such a thing?

MORGAN
Exactly! Can't you see? He's trying to put his guilt
upon me.

ARTHUR
Silence, Morgan! Let him answer.

LANCELOT
Because she wishes to hurt you, Arthur. What you are
doing now is just what she wants. She means to destroy
everything that you hold dear.

GUINEVERE
Of course, I remember now. Morgan it was you who
imprisoned me. I was frozen to the spot — cold as ice
in body and mind.

MORGAN
Don't worry, my dear, you will soon be very much
warmer.

ARTHUR
I said be silent, Morgan! Why should she wish to do
these things?

LANCELOT
Tell him, Morgan.

MORGAN
I am bid to be quiet.

LANCELOT
Then I will tell. Arthur, Morgan is your sister.

ARTHUR
What!

LANCELOT
Your half-sister. Your mother was also hers.

ARTHUR
I don't believe you.

LANCELOT
It is true. She hates you because your father killed
her father.

ARTHUR
My father would never do such a thing. Sir Ector is an
honourable man.

LANCELOT
I mean your real father.

ARTHUR
But I don't even know who he was.

LANCELOT
He was King Uther. He committed the most vile sin of
murder and then married his victim's wife. And thus it
was that you were born to be King.

ARTHUR
I cannot believe all of this.

LANCELOT
Ask Merlin. It was he who aided Uther in his dreadful
undertaking.

ARTHUR
Now I know that you are not telling the truth. Merlin
would never be involved in such a thing.

LANCELOT
But he was. Morgan has blackmailed him into silence all
this while.

ARTHUR
NO! You are a liar!

LANCELOT
Ask him, Arthur.

ARTHUR
Merlin! I know that you are always with me and will be
to the end of time. Say that this is not true.

MERLIN ON TAPE
Alas I cannot. To my eternal shame — It is true.

ARTHUR
Then everything is lost. Everything I have ever
believed in is false — a sham. The very walls of
Camelot should disappear and the Round Table be cast
into the fire. *(He breaks down)*

MORGAN
You have no idea what it was like. My life went from
bad to worse while yours went from strength to strength
— cosseted in your new home, with an influential Knight
for a father. I watched you become rich beyond measure,
while I languished in the realm of a broken and penni-
less King with nothing but bad debts for company. How I
hated you.

ARTHUR
If only I had listened to you, Lancelot. You warned me
but I gave no credit to your fears. And if only I had
gone myself to rescue Guinevere.

GUINEVERE
It doesn't matter, Arthur. I love you — that is all
that counts now.

ARTHUR
And I love you ... but nothing can ever be the same
again.

LANCELOT
It doesn't have to be like that. Merlin has repented of
the wrong he has done ... Who do you think it was told
me of all this? He has made amends just in time to save
Guinevere and Camelot. Release Guinevere and condemn
Morgan to the flames instead.

ARTHUR
No. Morgan shall live. She has done me great harm and
yet I understand how badly life has treated her. There
has been enough suffering. I will pardon her.

MORGAN
But why ... why should you do that?

ARTHUR
If you really are my sister, then you must live to earn
the honour of that title. You have a place here at
Camelot with us — should you wish it.

MORGAN
Thank you.

ARTHUR
Guinevere, my love, I hope that you can forgive my
thoughts and actions toward you.

GUINEVERE
My darling Arthur, of course I can. Just so long as you
release me from this bonfire!

ARTHUR
You shall be set free at once.

GALAHAD
Does that mean I can blow this taper out. *(Just as he
says this it burns down to his fingers and he drops it
on the wood.)* Ouch! *(The fire catches quickly)* Oh hec!

Loud sound of fire.

GUINEVERE
Help me!

ARTHUR
Sir Lancelot, quickly!

LANCELOT
I am with you, Sire.

Both men dodge the flames to untie Guinevere.

GUINEVERE
Quickly, the flames are getting closer.

LANCELOT
There is no way out, the fire surrounds us.

GALAHAD
Oh well, here we go!

He beats out a path to them and they all escape.

ARTHUR
Guinevere, are you all right?

GUINEVERE
Oh Arthur! *(They embrace)*

LANCELOT
Well done, Sir Galahad! Your bravery has saved our lives. You could have been killed.

GALAHAD
Oh hec! *(He faints)*

All exit.

MERLIN ON TAPE
And so Arthur and Guinevere were reconciled, Morgan promised to repent and Lancelot resumed his place at Court. But happy ever after was not in sight. Mordred and his mighty army were poised ready to storm the gates of Camelot. The two sides were evenly matched and fearing great bloodshed and anxious to redeem myself, I intervened. I persuaded Mordred to meet Arthur in single combat. One man pitched against the other with Camelot and all of Britain as the prize. My magic could not take sides in this. I, like you, could only stand aside and hope with all my might that truth and justice would prevail.

11. A ROPE BRIDGE ACROSS A WATERFALL

Very loud sound of falling water.

Mordred and Arthur enter from opposite sides.

MORDRED
So, King Arthur, we meet at last.

ARTHUR
Mordred, I wish that I could welcome you to Camelot but you are not welcome here, Sir.

MORDRED
Indeed! That is a pity, as I do not intend to leave.
For, whether I am welcome to Camelot or not, I mean to
take it.

ARTHUR
You will have to kill me first.

MORDRED
With pleasure! And, after I have killed you, your
mighty Kingdom and everything in it will be mine.

ARTHUR
Then prepare to be disappointed for I will not yield.

MORDRED
You will have no choice. And the greatest prize that
you shall yield to me, with value beyond Camelot
itself, will be your Queen — Guinevere.

ARTHUR
Then, sir, my fight will be even more determined. For
that, above all other, I cannot give. You must prepare
to die.

They fight. Mordred is killed but Arthur is badly injured.

Guinevere and Lancelot enter and run to him.

GUINEVERE
My Lord, you are hurt.

ARTHUR
Only my body is hurt, my love. My heart is sound, for
both you and Camelot are safe. Mordred is dead and his
evil can threaten us no more.

LANCELOT
I will send for a physician, Sire, to attend to your
wounds.

ARTHUR
No, my friend. My injuries will require more than mortal hand to heal them.

GUINEVERE
Arthur, please don't say such things. You are frighten-
ing me.

ARTHUR
Hush ... hush ... do not fear, for all will be well.
Sir Lancelot, you must take me to a boat and cast us
upon the waters of the lake.

LANCELOT
But where shall we be bound.

                    ARTHUR
Just do as I say, Lancelot ... please.
Lancelot, stop rowing.

                    LANCELOT
Your Majesty, we are in open water still.

                    ARTHUR
Take Excalibur and hold it above the water of the lake.
Its job is done and my Quest is over. It must be
returned safely home.

                    LANCELOT
But, Sire.

                    ARTHUR
Just do as I say.

*Lancelot does so and the Lady of the Lake appears, takes the
sword and then vanishes with it.*

Lancelot continues to row until:

12. AVALON

                    GUINEVERE
Where is this place?

                    ARTHUR
It is known as Avalon. This is where you must leave me.

                    LANCELOT
But my Lord.

                    GUINEVERE
Arthur, no!

                    ARTHUR
You must both be strong. Here I must stay until I am
healed and whole again.

                    GUINEVERE
But when will that be?

                    ARTHUR
I do not know. My job is done. Britain is safe and
strong. I shall remain here until I am needed and then,
in whatever guise, I shall return.

                    GUINEVERE
Then will I see you again?

ARTHUR
Oh yes, my love. In this life or the next ... for real love never dies and although great distances of time and space may separate us, our hearts shall never be apart.

Merlin enters.

MERLIN
With this my story ends ... or does it? King Arthur, the greatest King that ever lived, dwells peacefully in Avalon still. But the day will come when this land will call again for his leadership. At that time, when all will seemingly be lost, then Arthur will return and honour, truth and justice will reign supreme once again.

The final curtain.

FURTHER READING

Bicât, T. and Baldwin, C. (eds), *Devised and Collaborative Theatre* (The Crowood Press, 2002)

The Encyclopaedia Britannica

Hartnoll, P., *The Theatre (A Concise History)* (Thames & Hudson, 1998)

Hester, J., *Stage Acting Techniques* (The Crowood Press, 2004)

Lloyd Evans, G. and B., *Companion to Shakespeare* (JM Dent & Sons, 1990)

Perry, J., *The Rehearsal Handbook* (The Crowood Press, 2001)

Potter, N. (ed.), *Movement for Actors* (Allworth Press, 2002)

Rodenburg, P., *The Right to Speak* (Methuen, 1991)

Stanislavski, C., all his books (Methuen)

INDEX